ON
THE
THRESHOLD

The Report of the Bishops' Conference
Working Party
on Sacramental Initiation

Acknowledgements

The Scripture quotations contained herein are from the New Revised Standard Version: Catholic Edition copyright © 1989 by the Division of Christian Education of the National Council of the Churches of Christ in the U.S.A. Used by permission, All rights reserved.

Extracts from *The Church in the Modern World* (Gaudium et Spes) Vatican II Pastoral Constitution, December 1965. *Vatican Council II: The Conciliar and Post-conciliar Documents*, ed. Austin Flannery, OP, © 1975 Dominican Publications, Dublin.

Extracts from *Evangelisation in the Modern World* (Evangelii Nuntiandi), Apostolic Exhortation of Pope Paul VI, December 1975. Published by the Catholic Truth Society.

Extracts from *Catechesis in Our Time* (Catechesi Tradendae), Apostolic Exhortation of Pope John Paul II, October 1979. Published by the Catholic Truth Society.

Extract from *Christifideles Laici*, Apostolic Exhortation of Pope John Paul II, December 1986. Published by the Catholic Truth Society.

Extract from *Guidelines*, Jim Gallagher SDB, © 1986 Department of Christian Education and Formation, Bishops' Conference of England and Wales.

Extracts from the introduction to the *Rite of Christian Initiation of Adults*, © 1987, by the International Committee on English in the Liturgy, Inc. All rights reserved.

Extracts from *Adult Catechesis in the Christian Community* © 1990 by Libreria Editrice Vaticana, used by permision.

Extracts from the *Catechism of the Catholic Church*, English translation for the United Kingdom © 1994 Geoffrey Chapman-Libreria Editrice Vaticana, used by permission.

Extracts from the *General Directory for Catechesis* © 1997 by Liberia Editrice Vaticana, used by permision.

© 2000 Bishops' Conference of England and Wales

First published 2000

Published on behalf of the Bishops' Conference of England and Wales by Matthew James Publishing Ltd. 19 Wellington Close, Chelmsford Essex CM1 2EE

ISBN 1 898366 66 7

Cover and layout design by Peter Robb
Typeset by Linda East
Printed by J. W. Arrowsmith Ltd, Bristol

It has been my privilege to be part of the Working Party which has produced this Report.

In recent years the Bishops' Conference of England and Wales has explored what it means to proclaim the gospel in a changing world. A series of Reports, such as "The Sign We Give", "The Common Good" and "Valuing Difference", have looked at how the Church might respond to the challenges we face today. The sacramental life of the Church has also received attention with the publication of "One Bread, One Body".

This Report, initially proposed by the RCIA (Rite of Christian Initiation of Adults) National Network, is a further exploration, this time looking at our patterns of initiation.

There is much in "On the Threshold" which I believe can enrich us as we seek to share Good News with those who come to us seeking initiation. There is much to make us think and much to help us take positive, practical steps forward.

The Report was approved unanimously by the Bishops' Conference. It is a timely Report which I believe will help us all as we seek to journey together into the future.

✝ Brian Noble
Bishop of Shrewsbury

Crossing over the threshold into a new building can be both exciting and uncomfortable. It can be exciting because we are moving into a new place. It can be uncomfortable because we may be unsure about what we may discover. The word "threshold" has long been used as a symbol for moving from one way of life into another or from one way of thinking to another.

In our day and age many people now stand on the threshold of our Church. They have many questions. Do I really want to go in? Will there be someone to open the door to me? What will stepping over the threshold involve? Might I feel trapped? Do I really want to be here anyway? Would I rather walk away? Will I be made welcome? If I walk away now will I ever be able to come back? Whether it is on the presbytery doorstep or at the church or at the school entrance, standing on the threshold can be a nerve wracking experience, especially for those who, for whatever reason, do not feel at home in a church situation.

The local church community, perhaps represented by the priest, the catechist or the teacher, also stands on the threshold. When we meet those who come knocking on our doors asking for initiation for themselves or their children, we too have questions. How are we to respond to them? Should we welcome them with open arms and no pre-conditions or should we make certain demands? If so, what terms of membership should be required?

Yet standing on the threshold means more than this. Thresholds are not just places where others stand. We stand there too. It is not only those who come to us who pause on the threshold with all their questions, indecision and uncertainty. We also stand there. To really meet and stand with others on the threshold means to open ourselves up to our own sense of brokenness and vulnerability. This should not surprise us because it is doing what Jesus did; making himself vulnerable as he met people in order to offer them the way to new life and freedom.

A great deal has been written about the subject of initiation in recent decades. The Second Vatican Council (in the 1960's) decided to restore the *Rite of Christian Initiation of Adults (RCIA)* and to establish a *Rite of Christian Initiation of Children (RCIC)*, and these were published in 1972. Since then great efforts have been made in England and Wales to develop a better understanding of what is involved in initiating someone into the life of the Church. An RCIA Network has been established to help those responsible for developing this "new" approach, to reflect on their experience and offer mutual support. Baptism preparation courses for parents have been developed and sacramental preparation programmes developed for First Communion and Confirmation. This growth in practice has, however, further contributed to our concerns surrounding initiation. Situations are constantly changing. Those on both sides of the threshold are perplexed and confusion continues to surround initiation and how best we should respond.

What are the limits of the Report?

Aware that the time had come for some issues to be explored more deeply, the Bishops' Conference of England and Wales, at the request of the RCIA Network, set up a working party. The aim was to:

"explore some theological and pastoral issues which arise in local and diocesan practice with regard to Christian initiation of children and adults, drawing especially on experience of the RCIA over the last twenty years and the reflection prompted by that experience."

It was not part of the remit of the working party to present possible resolutions or make specific recommendations to the Church in England and Wales about such topics as the age of confirmation or criteria for baptism. Rather the working party was requested to:

"present perspectives and suggestions to assist parishes and dioceses to develop their understanding and pastoral practice."

The Report attempts to do this by using a style and language which is easily accessible by people working at local level and by incorporating material for reflection and discussion *within* the text.

Who is the Report for?

This Report has been written for local reflection, whether at parish, deanery or diocesan level. It has been designed to be used especially by catechists, teachers, priests and those concerned with meeting people as they stand on the threshold seeking initiation for themselves or their children.

How should we use the Report?

1   There are five sections in the Report:

    1   WHERE DO WE STAND?
    2   HOW DO WE BELONG?
    3   WHAT ARE WE LOOKING FOR?
    4   WHEN IS THE RIGHT TIME?
    5   WHAT ABOUT OUR CATECHESIS?

2   Each section builds on the next so it is important to use the Report as a whole. There are three main parts to each section.

- **Looking at our situation** – which begins with a story which helps us to "root" our thinking. Looking at our situation is important because the Church does not exist in a vacuum. We need to try and understand the world today of which we are all a part and how its effects are felt by all of us, those who are not part of the Church and those of us who are.

- **What might God be saying** – which seeks to discern what God might be encouraging us to consider in the light of our situation.

- **What might God be asking us to do** – which uses a gospel passage as a means of exploring ways forward for our future work.

3   The questions or statements for reflection are an important part of the document. They are designed to help us see how what is explored relates to our local situation. They could, for instance, be used by a group of catechists at parish level or on a deanery or diocesan "study day". Those who are reading the Report alone can also use them. Taking time to pause and consider the implications of what is said is an important part of reading the document.

4   Within each chapter there are some insights from important Church documents. These are to be found in the boxes at appropriate places in the text. They are there to locate our report within the unfolding tradition of the Catholic Church. They are

also there as starting points to help those who want to look deeper into our tradition to do so. Whilst our report is written using inclusive language, some of the documents quoted use exclusive language and to be faithful to the original this has been retained.

And finally ...

There is a tendency in our society at large and in the Church to concentrate on the negative aspects of our present situation. It is the belief of the working party that today we have unparalleled opportunities for the gospel to be shared. The door, far from being shut, is wide open to a faithful, sensitive and relevant sharing of the riches of our faith. As we stand on the threshold with those who come seeking initiation we know Christ stands with us and will journey with us all into the fullness of life he promises.

WHERE DO WE STAND?

"But Peter was standing outside at the gate" (John 18:16)

Tom and Mary were looking at photograph albums. One of their youngest granddaughters had just gone off to University and it had prompted them to look back down the years. As they looked through the pictures they found it difficult to really believe they now lived in the same world. Reliving the childhood of their four offspring it all seemed like a different era. And in a way it was. Tom had left his home at fifteen. His father and his grandparents had never moved from their small community. Now Tom's children were scattered. The chance to travel, to live in different places and see the world would simply not have been possible in his young days.

Mary had left her home to marry Tom. It was expected that she would marry. 'Career girls' were practically unknown. She had never trained for a career that would last. In her day the path for girls and the path for boys was more or less set and the educational system backed it up. When she was young there were far more discrepancies between the opportunities given to boys and those given to girls. Not that Mary would have changed her life. Her marriage to Tom had had its ups and downs, its difficulties, stresses and strains but they had stuck with it and now lived in the sort of companionable way which only couples devoted to each other seem to manage. She watched her children and grandchildren and knew that they were living in a world she, in her youth, would never have dreamed possible. They had chances to make decisions for themselves, to be themselves and could make of their lives what they wanted to make of them. She still found it difficult to believe that some of *her* children had gone to university. Even Anthony, her youngest, for whom school had been a real trial and who had got into considerable difficulty as a result of his anti-school attitude, had found a niche at last. After a succession of casual jobs and periods of unemployment he had set himself up in business as a gardener, something he had done since his childhood and at which he was really good. It was also a sign of the times that his older brothers and sister, who had gone on to higher education, praised him for his decision and his guts in stepping out on his own. There was no looking down on him, or criticism or patronising because he was not academically brilliant. They were prime examples of an attitude in society which was much more flexible, open and less class-ridden than in her youth.

Even though all their children but one had 'lapsed' from the practice of their faith Mary knew deep down that what she and Tom had sown and nurtured had not disappeared. Her four were good people whose sense of justice and concern for others was only too evident. Only yesterday she had heard all four of them (for once they were all at home together – a very rare occurrence) talking about the proposed plans to build on green belt land not far away. There was much talk about the environment which developed into a heated conversation about whose responsibility it all was and the dangers of short term gain at the expense of what Anthony called the 'long term respect we should have for creation'. And she knew they had been talking about God too – the grandchildren had been telling her.

Mary never said any of this to Tom, who likewise never spoke to Mary about his own assessment of the world in which they, their children and their grandchildren lived. Deep down he was less optimistic. Nothing seemed secure any more. The roles between men and women were blurred (and Tom was not at all sure it was a good thing) and nothing seemed to last either. The grandchildren wanted more and more things and forgot, or threw away, their new toys within a few weeks. It all had to be instant. They wanted it now.

Tom reflected that people took on board what they wanted to take on board and 'picked' what they liked. There was a lot of talk about rights but what about responsibilities? No one knew where they stood – everyone's opinion was as right as anyone else's and 'success' was defined as those who had the toughness to get to the top, even if it meant trampling over other people. No one, or at least only a few, took any notice of religion. Most of his children no longer practised the faith in which they had been brought up, though some of his grandchildren had been baptised and made their First Communion. He often felt guilty about this but had no idea what, if anything, could be done.

Pause & Reflect

What do you think are the positive and negative aspects of the world in which we live today?

I LOOKING AT OUR SITUATION

Tom and Mary and their family are not unusual. When people come to us for the sacraments of Baptism, Confirmation or First Communion for their children they do not come from a vacuum. Nor do those who come asking questions or seeking to become members of the Church as adults come as blank pages of a book. They, like us, are part

"We must be aware of and understand the aspirations, the yearnings, and the often dramatic features of the world in which we live. At all times the Church carries the responsibility of reading the signs of the time and of interpreting them in the light of the Gospel, if it is to carry out its task."
Vatican II The Church in the Modern World, 4

of the world which, whether we like it or not, shapes us all. The world has changed radically and quickly over recent years. If we are to find the best way to help people approach these sacraments of initiation we have no option but to look at the experiences of life, the values and the ideas they are bringing with them. If we can do this we shall be better equipped to meet them with the gospel message which makes sense to them and which helps them to a positive response.

Those who come knocking on the door asking for the sacraments cannot leave behind the real life situations which shape them, any more than we can leave behind what shapes us. So what major aspects of society might be influencing the attitudes they come with, and what does being aware of these demand of us in our response to them? To look at these is an essential pre-requisite of everything else. Here are some of those aspects and attitudes:

Today's society is *pluralistic*. There are many cultures, many groups, many views. Christianity is regarded by many people as simply *one* of these 'options'. And within Christianity there is cultural diversity too. We can no longer assume that people have much, if any, knowledge or experience of Christianity when they ask for baptism of their children. One of our problems is that we are still operating as if people *do* have a basic knowledge and experience of the faith. In fact, we are no longer in a 'Christendom situation' in these islands but *we are often still operating in our local parishes as if we are.*

a pluralistic society

> "*Many communities and individuals are called to live in a pluralistic and secularised world, in which forms of unbelief and religious indifference may be encountered together with vibrant expressions of religious and cultural pluralism. ... In these circumstances, a catechesis of evangelisation becomes indispensable: a catechesis which must be impregnated with the spirit of the Gospel and imparted in language adapted to the times and to the hearers.*"
>
> General Directory for Catechesis, 193-194

What happens as a result of this is that when people come to us for the sacraments of initiation we make assumptions which might not be correct; and when we make these assumptions we are not always starting from the right place. We do not have a common meeting point or we might not use the right language. They may not be able to really understand what we are saying because we are coming from different places with no common basis. They come to us with all sorts of expectations and ideas. We meet them with expectations and ideas of our own. There needs to be some common ground, a threshold or doorstep on which we both stand so that we can communicate with each other.

◆

*pick and
mix society*

◆

*we stand on
thresholds*

◆

*searching for
God on the
boundaries*

Today's society is less ordered and clearly defined than was once the case. People *pick and choose* what they want to believe – and they may 'pick up and put down' particular parts of their chosen faith. So people may come to us having already decided which 'bits' of the Church's life and practice they are willing to adopt, and which bits they have no intention of taking on board. It is a natural result of our 'pick and mix' attitude to life today. We, of course, want people to take seriously all the essential ingredients of the faith and this causes all sorts of tensions in them and in us too.

Pause & Reflect

What do you think are two of the major problems with a 'pick and mix' approach to Catholicism and what opportunities for a new approach might they present?

When people come to meet us asking for the sacraments of initiation they may well be uncertain or unsure what they want and why they want it. Alternatively, they may be very clear, but not always with the reasons we would like to hear, (e.g. coming for Baptism to get a place in a Catholic school). In a way they, and we, are meeting each other on a *threshold*. It will not be the only threshold in their lives. We all have these. Every time we move from one place to another, one stage of life to another, one form of lifestyle to another, we are crossing over thresholds. Each bereavement, new job, redundancy, new school, leads us over a threshold to something new. We may be both excited and fearful at these times. Moving over these thresholds is something which happens in the modern world with far greater frequency than in previous generations. Sometimes people may find themselves on the threshold of belief. It's exhausting to be always on the move physically or emotionally and people often long for security or something solid to hang on to. The sense of the sacred and the search for something to make sense to life is very strong in our society. People may not explicitly call this a search for God but it is an open door for the Church's message. This search for God, or however the search is expressed, is a desire for meaning and depth in what is often experienced as an increasingly shallow, depthless society. However, rarely do people equate this as having anything to do with the 'Church'.

Pause & Reflect

Name three *attitudes* (not actions), which we need to develop
if we are to meet people as they stand on various thresholds.

Some of the values of society today are *not gospel-friendly*. The belief
that being successful is what counts, the gathering of material
possessions, consumerism and the need to be seen as ever young –
what we might call society's 'divinization' of youth – are not gospel
values. Those who do not manage to attain these and many other
things experience a sense of oppression. People are not succeeding
where they feel they should succeed and they often feel guilty as a
result, or compelled to try harder. The Church, of course, has a
different view. Success is not about worldly possessions or status but
this message runs so counter to the prevailing attitude in society that
it is difficult for people to hear this message or they hear it only
negatively. Reticence to join wholeheartedly in the life of the Church
may sometimes be because the Church does not appear to fulfil the
criteria for 'success' as many people define it.

That society is profoundly affected by the media is beyond question.
Not all of this is bad. We have the media to thank for thoughtful and
reasoned argument alongside the subjective and salacious. We have
the TV to thank for excellent educational programmes and for many
lonely people it provides a life-line. How far the media responds to
society or creates it is a moot point but we can see in it an attitude to
life which all too often bolsters consumerism, materialism and
unreflected judgements on people or events. The media portrays
certain individuals as idols to be admired or imitated. Others are seen
to be victims with whom we can identify.

The attitude to religion is sometimes judgmental, sometimes
uninformed, often taken out of context; but frequently there is a
mismatch here.
Religion is somehow
seen as standing for
something 'other', yet
at the same time it is
ridiculed for being out
of touch, irrelevant or
just plain weird. The media want to have their cake and eat it.
Perhaps it is because the media still portrays religious people as

> *"... in addition to the numerous traditional means [of social
> communication] in use, the media has become essential for evangelisation
> and catechesis ... Good use of the media requires of catechists a serious
> commitment to knowledge, competence, training and up to date use of
> them."*
>
> General Directory for Catechesis, 160-161

◆
*counter-values
to the
gospel*

◆
*positive
and negative
aspects of
the media*

special or different that it comes down so heavily when such people go 'off the rails'. We live in a world profoundly affected by the media and we need to take account of these developments.

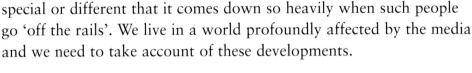

mobile – physically and mentally

People in today's society are *far more mobile* than in previous generations. Physically people move frequently. No longer is it common for people to live in the same area for the whole of their lives or, if they do, they are used to travelling often long distances. People are more mobile in their jobs too, or lack of them. And people are more mobile in their ideas and their opinions – often changing them frequently and quite radically – and sometimes back again. There is mobility in terms of roles too. There is no longer a set pattern about who does what. Some of the change is positive and long overdue. The subordination of women in our society is largely, though by no means completely, seen to be unacceptable. Racial or religious prejudice or discrimination on the grounds of ability or background is likewise condemned. Some of the changes are less helpful. More mobility can lead to loss of commitment to a particular group, society or Church, or a sense of insecurity, 'lostness' and shallowness. But mobility in all its forms is here to stay and the Church cannot ignore it or pretend it is not happening.

an individualistic society

One of the most startling aspects of modern society is *individualism*. This process began long ago but has become more obvious in recent years. "I" and "my" are seen to be more important than "we" and "our". This individualism is expressed in phrases such as "I have rights", "it's my life", "I come first", "it's my belief", "I can be a Christian without going to church." In many ways this sense of self was long overdue but what is missing is that today it is often not connected with any sense of community. This is a real problem for the Church which believes faith is a communal as well as a personal affair. That we become more truly our real selves in the context of our relationships with others and with God is difficult for people to hear. Even in the Church we have always known this danger. But society is pushing us towards even greater individualism. No one would deny that there is a place for private prayer or for 'recharging the spiritual batteries' by finding time to reflect on one's own, but if this is *all*

> "The pace of change is so far-reaching and rapid nowadays that no one can allow himself to close his eyes to the course of events or indifferently ignore them and wallow in the luxury of a merely individualistic morality. The best way to fulfil one's obligations of justice and love is to contribute to the common good ...»
>
> Vatican II The Church in the Modern World, 30

there is then a central element of the Catholic faith – namely that we are part of a family – is missing.

All this and much more leaves us in the Church with a sense of the 'messiness' of things and with many questions with regard to initiation, with many tensions and uncertainties about how to handle pastoral situations. We shall be exploring many of these in the pages which follow but here are a few tensions which the 'signs of the times' create:

- the individualism of modern society – the communality of the Church
- the importance of fashion in our culture – the unchanging, permanent gospel
- the Church existing within the world – the Church as different to the world
- people wanting to receive something from the Church – people not wanting to be committed to it
- 'Church' language – the everyday language of people
- the expectations of people coming for initiation – the expectations of the Church

Pause & Reflect

What three practical problems do we experience as a believing community committed to each other in an individualistic society?

What other tensions do you see arising directly from our situation today?

2 WHAT MIGHT GOD BE SAYING?

What then might God be saying to us as we look at our world today? Whatever we may think of today's society, its good and bad points, we are called by God to look within it. This is not an optional extra. The wonder and the grief, the uncertainties and the yearnings of those who come and stand on the threshold

> *"The joy and hope, the grief and anguish of the men of our time, especially of those who are poor or afflicted in any way, are the joy and hope, the grief and anguish of the followers of Christ as well."*
>
> Vatican II The Church in the Modern World, 1

of the Church with us are our joys and sorrows too. In initiating individuals into the Body of Christ, the Church cannot *but* be affected

discover where God is at work

the right sort of approach

by all the cultural influences which determine much of what is seen as worthy of joy, hope, sorrow or anxiety in society. In other words, as we have seen, we are part of our culture and God is calling us to attend to what shapes people's vision of life in order to help them make sense of the gospel for themselves. There are two practical results of this attitude.

First, *God is at work in people's lives* – our task is to help them see where God is present and what God is calling them to be and do. We cannot do this ignoring the values and vision they have as we meet them on the threshold.

Secondly, in order to help people make sense of the gospel for themselves and to respond to God's offer which lies within the sacraments of initiation we need to ask *what sort of approach* God may be asking us to adopt. Is it an approach which treats people with all the dignity with which God treats them? In other words we need to treat people as adults coming with life experience in which God has already been active whether they have recognised this or not.

> *"The fundamental importance is the dialogical approach which, while recognising that all are called to the obedience of faith, (Rom 1:5), respects the basic freedom and autonomy of adults and encourages them to engage in an open and cordial dialogue. In this way they can make known their needs and participate, as they should, as subjects or agents in their own catechesis and that of others."*
>
> Adult Catechesis in the Christian Community: Some Principles and Guidelines, 57

Pause & Reflect

How can we help people see where God is active in our world?

talk about the gospel before sacraments

One of the things God may be saying to us in the light of our present situation is to realise afresh the need to *talk about the gospel before we talk about sacraments*. The concern that we sacramentalise before we evangelise has been around in the Church in these countries for some time, but in our action we are often beginning as if people had already stepped over the threshold when they are only knocking on the door.

We have seen that society has less cohesiveness and fewer commonly acknowledged boundaries than was once the case. It is now up to each individual to decide many things which in previous generations may have been decided for him or her. Even if this was not the case there were certain over-arching parameters recognised by society against which a decision could be measured. This has left many people with a *genuine sense of lostness or uncertainty*. We are a fragmented society and the Church exists within this fragmentation. There are two ways the Church can respond to this. We can either offer the certainties we hold in an exclusive way or we can offer the same certainties in a different, more open, way. The image of Jesus on the cross can help us here. This is a Jesus willing to be at the mercy of the world around him but by his very vulnerability he brings us home, makes us at-one with God. The joy of the resurrection comes through the brokenness and tension of the cross. In practice this means that we, his people, have to be like him, being prepared for brokenness.

As we reflect on this perhaps God is saying to us that the way to help people experience that joy is for us to be willing to *enter the brokenness of their lives* and the life of the world in which we all live. This means listening to people without judging them; standing with them when faith is difficult and celebrating with them those joys they experience. Entering the pain of people's lives is bound to be painful for us too. People will sometimes reject us (just as they rejected Jesus) or they will say the Church should stand apart from the 'messiness' of this broken world and limit itself to 'spiritual things'. But if we did that we would not be true to the gospel which is about God taking on board our messy human condition in Jesus. This way of thinking will entail an image of Church different to what we sometimes imagine. This is a Church which, sure of its message, is not afraid to be vulnerable, standing in the world for the sake of the world. Doing this is *not* bowing to those aspects of contemporary culture which are not gospel-affirmed. It is enabling the Word to be made flesh with all the vulnerability of the stable and the cross knowing that a new beginning, a new culture, for individuals and societies is thus in the process of creation. It is an invitation to find a new way to be Church in our fragmented, broken world. In practice it means taking a flexible approach, living with failure and an openness to see God at work where we might not expect.

Finally, what is God saying to us about *change*? Change is difficult for us as individuals and as communities. On the one hand we might glimpse the opportunities which a change of perspective or action

❖

responding to uncertainty...

❖

coping with change

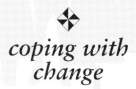

might offer. On the other we fear to let go and move forward lest we lose something important, not realising that we always take the past with us. Yet we are asking for change in those who come to us. Is not God asking change of us too? We are called not only to evangelise but to be evangelised ourselves and, whenever we hear God afresh, we must be prepared to shift gears.

> *"The Church is an evangeliser but she begins by being evangelised herself. She has a constant need of being evangelised if she wishes to retain freshness, vigour and strength in order to proclaim the gospel."*
>
> Evangelisation in the Modern World, 15

God, then, might be asking us to think about:
- Discovering where God is at work in people's lives
- Finding an appropriate approach
- Talking about the gospel before we talk about sacraments
- Entering the brokenness and tension of people's lives
- How we might be asked to change

Pause & Reflect

What strikes you as important from these ideas?

3 WHAT MIGHT GOD BE ASKING US TO DO?

We have looked briefly at the world we are all in. We have thought about what God might be saying to us. So what might God be asking us to do? Looking at this account from St Luke's gospel of how Jesus dealt with his own world can help us see what God might be calling us to do in the light of our own situation and what we have discerned so far. Read the text carefully and underline any words which stand out for you.

> *On one occasion when Jesus was going to the house of a leader of the Pharisees to eat a meal on the sabbath, they were watching him closely. Just then, in front of him, there was a man who had dropsy. And Jesus asked the lawyers and Pharisees, "Is it lawful to cure people on the sabbath, or not?" But they were silent. So Jesus took him and healed him, and sent him away. Then he said to them, "If one of you has a*

child or an ox that has fallen into a well, will you not immediately pull it out on a sabbath day?" And they could not reply to this.

(Luke 14:1-6)

There are five things to notice about this text.

1   Jesus was in a tense situation. The Pharisees were watching him closely. All through his ministry he had to face tensions of one sort or another. Each situation had to be taken individually. Different people and groups expected different things from him and came with different questions, needs and opinions; just as people stand on the threshold with us with the whole range of different expectations, needs and opinions when they come for the sacraments of initiation. Jesus always *lived with these tensions*. He did not pretend they did not exist or try to cover them over. Rather he always tried to use them creatively.

❖

live with the tensions

Q   Can you think of other instances when Jesus lived with tension?
How can we learn to live with the tensions we experience with regard to those coming for sacramental initiation?

2   Jesus is *creative* with the position in which he finds himself. There is a sense of anticipation in this story. What will he do? How will he handle the tension? How will he be both true to his tradition (the Jewish law) and yet not be a slave to it? How will he deal with the need to retain the Law and yet not be burdened by it? Which comes first, the Law or the sick man? As always Jesus meets people *where they are* – on their 'home ground'. He uses what they are familiar with, in this case the law, as a tool to get his message across. He is creative with each situation he encounters and is always on the lookout for signs of hope.

❖

be creative

– meet people where they are

Q   What *sort of attitude* is necessary if we are to engage creatively with people?

3   When Jesus meets this situation his words to the lawyers and Pharisees are based on what he knows they know. In other words he meets them *with their own language*. He uses what they know best to make his point, a question about the law: "Is it permitted

– use the right language

19

*– through the
lens of Jesus*

to heal on the Sabbath day or not?" Using the right language with people is not only helpful but essential.

Q   When talking to people about initiation what words or phrases do you think need 'translating'?

4   Whenever Jesus acts and talks like this people's views about him change. He also provokes them to reassess their own view of the world. We do not know, in this instance, what reaction he got but we know that on other occasions he was met with hostility by some and welcomed by others. Often the same incident brought forth both reactions. As we look at the world around us it is part of the task of the parish to help us see things 'through the lens' of Jesus. In other words to help *us* form a *new way of looking at things*. When people come to us for sacramental initiation we want them to begin to see things differently too but they can only do this if we ourselves have "eyes to see and ears to hear". We are in this together.

Q   Can you think of one thing which would help people in our parishes look at the world differently?

5   Finally, Jesus here is engaging with his own people but the man before him is also sick. Sickness was seen in Jesus' time as a result of sin and therefore, technically, this man was viewed as a sinner, removed from what we might call 'the fullness of the faith community'. Such people lived in a different culture. But this does not stop Jesus making contact with him and healing him.

✦

*cultural
diversity*

We know from all the gospels that Jesus is open to mixing with anyone and everyone, often being condemned for it, and as such he moved between cultures. He was well aware of what today we would call 'cultural diversity' and was not afraid nor limited by it. Indeed, he often *celebrated* with the sort of people no self-respecting Rabbi should ever have associated with. Cultural diversity is a mark of our age and it is seen in those who stand on the thresholds of our Church communities. They challenge us. How are we to react to them? How are we to celebrate the good things which cultural diversity brings?

Q   What diversity do you see in people who come to your
     Church to celebrate the sacraments of initiation?

We have looked briefly at the world in which we as Church exist, at
what God might be saying and at a few ways in which we might
respond. Let us now have a closer look at the theme of what it means
to belong to the Church in this new age, at the difficulties and the
possibilities which belonging presents to us.

HOW DO WE BELONG?

*"When I came to Troas to proclaim the good news of
Christ, a door was opened for me in the Lord"*

(2 Corinthians 2:12)

Tom and Mary had been members of the congregation of St Oswald's
since they moved into the area over 20 years ago. Their children had gone to
the parish primary school and then on to the local Catholic secondary
school. Tom was a leading light in the SVP and, like Mary, was a Minister of
Communion. Mary was active in the local CAFOD group and a member of
the diocesan Justice and Peace Commission. They were both involved in their
local "Churches Together" council – their interest in ecumenism had really
begun when Paul, their son, became engaged to Anne, a non-Catholic who
had since been received into the Church through the parish RCIA process.

Paul and Anne were now living at the other end of the country and
were active in the life of their local parish. Tom and Mary's other children had
different attitudes to the Church. If asked they would all say they 'belonged',
but what that belonging meant to each of them varied.

Anthony, the youngest, had no real connection with the Church. His
belonging was through his past and his parents. He believed in God but he
did not think this necessarily meant he had to belong to any church. He still
filled in "RC" on forms which asked for his religious affiliation but he believed
he could lead a good Christian life on his own – not that he thought about it
very much.

Tracey had married Kevin, also a Catholic, at St Oswald's but they had
moved abroad and never become involved in the local church. When their
first child came along Tom and Mary assumed the Baptism would take place
reasonably soon. But nothing happened. Both of them wondered whether
they should mention Baptism or not. Tom felt more worried than Mary. He
still felt guilty and kept asking himself where he had gone wrong. Surely
Tracey knew enough to want Harry baptised. Tracey sometimes reflected on
this herself, but neither she nor Kevin had any intention of belonging to the
Church in an active way so it seemed better to let Harry make up his own
mind when he was old enough.

Peter had also
married and he and Kate
had two children. Both
had been baptised and
the eldest, Rebecca, was
now in the Catholic
school. Her parents were
concerned members of
the PTA and supportive of the school and some of the parish activities if
Rebecca was involved. But they never went to Mass on Sundays or went
only on special occasions. Kate was not a Catholic and that made for real

*"The Christian community cannot carry out a permanent catechesis without
the direct and skilled participation of adults, whether as receivers or
promoters of catechetical activity. The world in which the young are called
to live ... is governed by adults: the faith of these adults, too, should
continually be enlightened... [It is] no less necessary for adults than for
children."*

Catechesis in Our Time, 43

difficulties. They belonged on their own terms and made up their own minds about what and what not to take on board. Tom and Mary at least felt there was a chance Rebecca would get a "good Catholic education" but were still concerned. Surely children really needed to see their parent's involvement if they were to grow in faith.

It was only Anne and Paul who seemed to belong to the Church in what Tom and Mary thought of as "proper belonging" and that was largely because Anne, coming into the Church as an adult, had done so with a commitment that had carried Paul along with it. For that Mary and Tom gave heartfelt thanks.

Pause & Reflect

What different styles of belonging do you see in your parish?

1 LOOKING AT OUR SITUATION

Tom and Mary's family is not unusual. There are different views about belonging – and we know that we cannot look at initiation today unless we look at what we understand by belonging.

One of the difficulties we face with regard to initiation is that there are many ways of understanding what it means to belong. For some belonging means no more than having the baby baptised. For others it means regular attendance at Mass. Many of our tensions are due to these varying viewpoints. We have one understanding, others are coming from a different starting point.

Some people approach the Church requesting the sacraments of initiation for their children or for themselves but do not want to belong in anything other than a nominal way. Others want to belong on their own terms. There are still others who want to belong fully but for various reasons, such as divorce and re-marriage, cannot do so. The result of all this is that the link between belonging to the Church and the sacraments of initiation can be very strained.

Of course, much of this is not new. There have always been people who have come for the sacraments, but who have belonged in rather tenuous ways. What is different today is that the idea of what it means to belong to anything has changed.

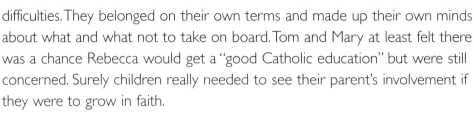

❖
people belong in different ways

Exploring what it means to belong and why some people find it difficult means exploring a number of tensions which are only too familiar in parish life. One of these is the tension between what the individual wants and what the community desires. There is an increased sense of individualism today. Our increased desire for self-fulfilment and individual rights is, in itself, positive but it often results in a tension between "what I want" and what the community requires. In society at large the sense of belonging does not always sit easily with the stress on "what I want, what I need and my rights." There is sometimes a clash between my rights and my responsibilities. This is very apparent with regards to the baptism of children whose families only loosely belong, but it is a part of a much larger pattern in society as a whole.

tensions –
rights and
responsibilities

Another aspect of modern society which impacts on our sacramental life is the tension which can exist between what we might call alienation and absorption. Most of us live with this tension. It is the tightrope stretched between not wanting to be on our own and being swamped by something bigger than ourselves. We do not want to be isolated but nor do we want to find ourselves merged into something too big for us. People want to be part of something but not absorbed by it. In practice we find that parents, young people and adults can approach the sacraments of initiation from two angles. They may want to celebrate this belonging, but they may also be overwhelmed by the thought that there is a level of belonging required which they fear is too much for them.

tensions –
alienation
and
absorption

> "Baptism is the sacrament of the faith. But faith needs the community of believers. It is only within the faith of the Church that each of the faithful can believe. The faith required for Baptism is not a perfect and mature faith, but a beginning that is called to develop."
>
> Catechism of the Catholic Church, 1253

There is another tension we need to consider when we think about belonging. To belong to the Church in a lived way is to be unlike most of our contemporaries. This sense of being different, and being seen to be different, is not comfortable. We want to be identified with the Church but at the same time do not want to be seen to be different. So there is the ever present danger of living on the margins of the Church, belonging but on our own terms.

tensions –
not wanting
to be
different

Pause & Reflect

How do these tensions show themselves in the life of our parish?

*the belonging
continuum*

Tensions such as these suggest that people are in different places on the belonging continuum. Some are moving towards a greater sense of belonging, some are moving away. There are others whose belonging is very tenuous – but who probably still call themselves Catholics – who live good and Christ-like lives. Finding out where people think they are on the "belonging line" is an important aspect of our initial contact with them.

We are all affected by the society in which we live and, because society is always changing, the threshold on which we meet people shifts too. This has always been the case. In the history of the Church 'belonging' has meant different things

> *"We can say of catechesis, as well as of evangelisation in general, that it is called to bring the power of the gospel into the very heart of culture and cultures."*
> Catechesis in Our Time, 53

at different times. Sometimes it has meant a deep commitment, the result of persecution. At other times a nominal sense of belonging was the norm because being baptised was what everybody underwent. In some periods of our history *not* to be baptised was to be different from society's norms. As we have seen, today the opposite is true. So for many people there is a desire to belong but not to belong, to want the sacraments but not the community involvement that goes with them. When people stand on the threshold – often literally at the

*learning
from history*

> *"The split between the gospel and culture is undoubtedly the tragedy of our time."*
> Evangelisation in the Modern World, 19

presbytery door – they are frequently standing on the edge of belonging.

2 WHAT MIGHT GOD BE SAYING?

If belonging means different things to the different people who approach us for the sacraments of initiation, what might God be saying in how we might respond. It might help us to answer this question by using an image from our physical world.

*ragged
edges*

Geologists tell us that the land masses of the earth are plates of continental crust. Sometimes these plates are pulled apart, sometimes one plate dives under another and sometimes two plates slide in opposite directions. Where these collisions take place the earth's crust is at its most creative. Mountains are formed, new land created. The earth is in a continual process of movement and that movement is at its most creative where the earth's crust is at its thinnest and where one plate meets another. This image may be helpful when we consider what God may be saying to us as we meet people on the thresholds of belonging.

One conclusion we can draw from this image of the tectonic plates of the earth's crust is that it provides us with images of Church. First, the plates are both solid *and* flexible. They are secure but also capable of movement. In our initiatory action as Church we should be aware both of the solidity and richness of our heritage, which gives us a secure base, *and* of the need to be flexible whenever we enter into dialogue with individuals.

A second image of Church we can draw from our knowledge of how new earth is created is to do with death and dying. New land is only formed where old land dies. The crust of one plate crashes into another, dives under it and disappears. In its place new territory is born. The eternal gospel is always in the process of being reborn. It never dies but the way in which we proclaim it sometimes needs to die in order that new beginnings can happen. We sometimes need to let go of some aspects of our life in order for new things to grow. Ways of preparing people for the sacraments which no longer communicate, or a language which no longer speaks, may need to die.

New territory can only be formed on the earth where old land dies. There are some people who, for one reason or another, feel the Church is "dead" for them. We tend to see this in entirely negative terms but it might be that God is calling us to look for the positive and see how new territory might be formed through our interaction with those who have lapsed from the practice of their faith. It may well be that their lapsing has been for them an emancipation from wrong and mistaken images of God or the Church. God has not ceased to be active and creative, so the potential for a new beginning may well be far more likely than we may have imagined. A new sense of belonging may well be in the process of being born.

But there is more to be gained from this geological image than ways of thinking about the Church. God might be inviting us to explore where we make contact with people. God's most creative action might well take place where "the crust is the thinnest." In other words where there are ragged edges. Being willing to meet people with all their ragged

images of church – secure and flexible

dying and rising

the lapsed... and new beginnings

at the margins

understanding of belonging may well be the most creative way. No movement on the earth happens where the crust is thick. All the creative activity takes place *at the margins*. Therefore, meeting people in *their* place of belonging, with all its imperfections, has the potential to create new territory for further exploration. We often expect to find God at the place where the crust is most solid, that is, where the Church is obvious, but often God is at work on the fringes.

Pause & Reflect

How can we best listen to people's "ragged edges of belonging" and respond?

flexibility

Meeting people with all their imperfections of belonging requires flexibility and willingness to adapt. If there are ragged edges in the perceptions of those who come to us about what belonging means, there need to be ways of responding to that raggedness which begins where people already are. What is required is a response

> Meeting people with all their imperfections of belonging reminds us of "the adaptation of doctrinal presentations and catechetical methods required by the differences of culture, age, spiritual maturity and social and ecclesial condition among all those to whom [catechesis] is addressed."
> Catechism of the Catholic Church, 24

which will 'dovetail' into the ragged edges. The danger is that what we offer is more like the thick crust of the earth, immovable and with a ready packaged position, than a thin, flexible crust which moves in response to the other. Although the latter may be untidy it is often also the most creative. Just as the earth very rapidly creates new territory at the place of encounter between two plates, so with people new 'land' may be created quite quickly where a true meeting happens. This is the joy of the real encounter.

Pause & Reflect

What would this flexible approach mean in practice?
What other ideas could be developed from the image of the tectonic plates?

3 WHAT MIGHT GOD BE ASKING US TO DO?

We have looked briefly at some of the aspects of belonging and about what God might be saying to us. Looking at this story from St Luke's gospel might help us see how we might respond. The story of Jesus meeting and healing the man living in the tombs is a story about Jesus moving to the edges, and it is also about ways of belonging.

(Jesus and the disciples) then arrived at the country of the Gerasenes, which is opposite Galilee. As he stepped out on land, a man of the city who had demons met him. For a long time he had worn no clothes, and he did not live in a house but in the tombs. When he saw Jesus, he fell down before him and shouted at the top of his voice, "What have you to do with me, Jesus, Son of the Most High God? I beg you, do not torment me" – for Jesus had commanded the unclean spirit to come out of the man. (For many times it had seized him; he was kept under guard and bound with chains and shackles, but he would break the bonds and be driven by the demons into the wilds.) Jesus then asked him, "What is your name?" He said, "Legion"; for many demons had entered him. They begged him not to order them to go back into the abyss.

Now there on the hillside a large herd of swine was feeding; and the demons begged Jesus to let them enter these. So he gave them permission. Then the demons came out of the man and entered the swine, and the herd rushed down the steep bank into the lake and was drowned. When the swineherds saw what had happened, they ran off and told it in the city and in the country. Then people came out to see what had happened, and when they came to Jesus, they found the man from whom the demons had gone sitting at the feet of Jesus, clothed and in his right mind. And they were afraid.

The man from whom the demons had gone begged that he might be with him; but Jesus sent him away, saying, "Return to your home, and declare how much God has done for you." So he went away, proclaiming throughout the city how much Jesus had done for him.

(Luke 8:26-35, 38-39)

There are four ideas we might work with from this story, all of which require a practical response.

1   The story begins with Jesus travelling into foreign territory. As such he is vulnerable in two ways. He is vulnerable to the reaction of

moving to the edges

29

those whom he does not know, the strangers he will meet. He is also vulnerable to those who would criticise him for his open approach. After all he is travelling in foreign and, in the culture of his time, unclean territory. The importance of this for us is that moving to the edges in our meeting with people can be uncomfortable. We cannot be sure of the reaction either by those seeking initiation, or of those who might find such an open approach difficult to understand.

Q What do we find frightening about taking a very flexible approach to those who are at different stages of belonging?

recognising Jesus and belonging

2 The man Jesus meets is pictured as disturbed and described in the story in terms of demons. Yet there is a clear recognition of who Jesus is. Despite everything the man and his sickness recognise Jesus. He stands for all those who may not belong in the traditional sense but who nonetheless believe. Jesus meets him – and us and our contemporaries – with all his (and our) doubts and beliefs, ignorance and knowledge, strengths and weaknesses.

"The catechist ... interprets the Church to those who are being catechised. The catechist reads and teaches them to read the signs of faith ... discern(s) and make(s) the most of the spiritual inklings already present in a person's spiritual life ..."

Pope John Paul II's address to the International Catechetical Congress, Oct '97 (inclusive version)

Q In practical terms how does this passage suggest we should encounter people who believe but do not belong?

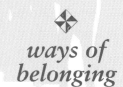

ways of belonging

3 We can presume this man was once part of his community but has now been excluded from it. After his healing he is sent back to that community, to be part of it again. "Go back home to your own people." There he encourages others to respond to Jesus by proclaiming what Jesus has done for him. He once left this community, now he rejoins and perhaps encourages others to join for the first time.

Q How do people experience exclusion from our community? How can they be re-integrated? How can the parish community sponsor those seeking initiation?

4   Finally, when we look at this story as a whole, we see that Jesus' action with this man is threefold. It is a model of good catechetical mentality and practice. He *goes* to him, *talks* to him and then *acts* to restore him.

First, Jesus *goes* to the man as the man goes towards Jesus. There is a mutual meeting place, and that place is on the margins, in unfamiliar territory. It is an encounter.

Secondly, Jesus *talks* to him. He asks him a question and the question is, "What is your name?" His words have a direct bearing on the condition in which Legion finds himself. It is real communication.

Thirdly, Jesus *acts*. This action is a *process*, not a one-off activity. After Legion's healing Jesus acts to give him a task and in so doing restores his dignity as well as his health.

Q   In what practical ways is our meeting with people, where ever they are on their belonging continuum, Jesus' model of encounter, communication and action?

> *"The discourse of faith with adults must take serious account of their experience, their conditioning and of the challenges which they have encountered in life. Their questions of faith as well as their needs are many and varied."*
>
> General Directory for Catechesis, 172

We have looked at the importance of belonging and what that means for the initiatory process. Now we turn to ways in which we currently initiate and ways we might explore for the future.

WHAT ARE WE LOOKING FOR?

"After this I looked and there, in heaven, a door stood open."

(Rev 4:1)

Tom and Mary were visiting Peter, Kate and the grandchildren. They were just settling down to an evening in front of the television when Peter came in. He slumped into an armchair, picked up the paper and gave it a cursory glance. He fidgeted, then he fiddled with the television remote control, flicking through the channels. Mary shot him a glance. With Peter she always knew when something was about to "blow". His body language gave him away.

"Where's Kate and Rebecca?" asked Mary. Peter muttered something uncharitable about the Church.

"All we want is for Rebecca to make her First Communion like I did," he said, "but now we've got to go to all these meetings. That's where they both are. And they'll be back with some homework we've all got to do or something. Personally I think it's way over the top."

"Why aren't you with them?" asked Tom. It was not a timely question as far as Peter was concerned.

"Because I don't see why I should," he exploded. "Why can't we just let the school do the preparation and all that stuff or those catechists, or whatever they're called, can do it? It's not as if we won't support her. We've got a great party lined up as you know and the white dress is on order. She'll look wonderful! But all these meetings and what not. I can't see the point."

Tom and Mary looked at each other. Neither of them knew quite what to say. They were delighted Rebecca was about to make her First Communion and to some extent they understood Peter's position. But the distance between what he thought about this sacrament of initiation and what the Church thought was enormous. Despite all that the parish had done to try and explain why they were operating in this way nothing seemed to have got through to Peter. They had no doubt he would be as proud as punch on the day, that he would probably remember it better than he remembered his own First Communion, but surely there was more to it for him than the white dress and the party.

At that moment Mary recalled the two photographs of Peter which hung on their bedroom wall at home. One was of Peter on his own First Communion day, smiling broadly, wearing his white shirt and red tie. The other showed him in his cub uniform on the day of his initiation into the pack. He smiled from this picture too but in this photograph he looked not just happy, he looked radiant. Mary couldn't help making comparisons. Peter had experienced two forms of initiation as a boy and perhaps the experience still lived with him. Perhaps his own First Communion had not meant much to him and that background was coming through in his attitude to Rebecca's First Communion. It was a sobering thought. It wasn't *all* Peter's fault, nor was it hers or Tom's, nor the Church's. Perhaps everyone still had a lot to learn.

Tom and Mary's story is not unusual. As we saw in the last chapter, there are various ways of belonging and different people are at different places on the "belonging continuum". In this chapter we look at what we are doing when we initiate and what lessons we can learn for the future.

Pause & Reflect

What are your memories of the various initiation rites you have experienced and why are they meaningful?
Why do you think Peter looked so different in the two photographs?

I   LOOKING AT OUR SITUATION

Every parish knows that there are times when preparing for and celebrating the sacraments of initiation can be one of the most profound and moving events the community experiences. Every parish also knows that there are times when the experience of celebrating these sacraments is anything but positive, when it all "falls flat" or there seems little, if any, communication going on.

Preparation for the sacraments can also be both a positive and negative experience in the parish. Sometimes it seems as if it fails to connect with people, sometimes it sparks. Why is this so? We can identify some particular reasons why these different positive and negative experiences are commonplace in our parish life. There are others but these are especially important.

✦
motives for initiation

One of the reasons for these different experiences is that people come to the Church for these sacraments with different motives. Most, if not all, are basically good. People may not be able to articulate *why* they want Baptism for their children, or First Confirmation or Communion, but they have a deep seated "gut feeling" that these are important and it is the right thing to do. Even those whose motives at first sight seem dubious are, at

"... many people have been baptised but lead lives entirely divorced from Christianity. ... even though in many hearts religious feeling has not been completely lost. Re-awakening these to the faith is a real challenge for the Church. There are, moreover, numerous other Christians, often highly educated, whose religious formation amounts solely to that which they received in childhood. These also need to re-examine and develop their faith from a different standpoint."

General Directory for Catechesis, 25

heart, basing them on something good. Parents whose motive for Baptism is to get their child into the Catholic school are, nonetheless, doing so because they want what they believe is the best for their child. However much we may wish things were different, these different motives are our starting point and it is with these that we have to work.

Another reason why some of our experiences with regard to preparation and celebration of the sacraments are not always positive is to do with what we might call a "supermarket mentality". In the supermarket we have a huge range of choices and we pick which product will suit us best or which will best suit our individual needs at any given moment. We have already noticed that society has adopted a "pick and mix" approach to almost everything, so it should come as no surprise to us that people bring this mentality with them to the Church. We all do. We take what we like and find it difficult to cope with what we don't like. So in our story Peter picks those parts of the First Communion process he likes and is not prepared to accept those parts he disagrees with or does not understand. Of course, for the sake of Rebecca, he will probably do anything but mentally he is picking and mixing. This creates real tensions for us as Church because sacraments are not products, though many people think and act as if they were.

❖

supermarket mentality

A third reason for our negative and positive experiences concerns the relationship between the individual and the community. We have already seen that individualism is an important factor in society so it is little wonder that people approach the Sacraments of Initiation asking "what is in it for me?" (or at least with this in the background). The stress we place on being part of the community, of belonging to the family of God with privileges and responsibilities, does not sit easily with the individualism of today. So, here too there is a tension we need to recognise.

❖

individual versus communal

"Catechetical pedagogy will be effective to the extent that the Christian community becomes a point of concrete reference for the faith journey of individuals."

General Directory for Catechesis, 58

A fourth reason for our difficulties concerns communication. We seem to have difficulty communicating with people and they often seem to have difficulty communicating with us. There are a number of reasons for this. Unfamiliarity with our ideas, feeling uncomfortable with our

❖

communication difficulties

ways of doing things and the language we use are all part of the problem. It is not just that people don't listen to us, it is also that we fail to listen to them and value what they say. This is just as important as using the right words or concepts which enable them to make connections with us. The risk is that we both speak but often don't understand each other. There is a breakdown of communication. Too often we are not on each other's wavelength, then we either give up on each other or go through the motions "on parallel lines".

> *"Evangelisation loses much of its force and effectiveness if it does not take into consideration the actual people to whom it is addressed, if it does not use their language, their signs, their symbols, if it does not answer the questions they ask and if it does not have an impact on their concrete life."*
>
> Evangelisation in the Modern World, 63

❖ the sacramental gap

This communication difficulty also applies to the images we use. There is often a gap between the sacramental world of the Church and the world of parents and children. The whole idea of the symbolic is central to us. We live with symbols, we speak symbolically, but what exactly does this mean to someone who is either new to the Church or re-discovering it?

One of our difficulties with regard to the use of symbols is that some "speak" to people but others do not. Some seem to have lost their meaning for most people. The problem here is that symbols, by their nature, speak to our depths. If we have to explain them they somehow lose their power. We might place a bunch of flowers at the place where someone died because "it seems right" or "it helped me to do something" but, if we have to try and explain our action, something of the power of the symbol is lost – the chances are we could not really explain it in words anyway. Symbols reach those parts of us words cannot. So if our symbols have lost this power or meaning for many people, we have a real difficulty. We ourselves have not helped matters because we as Church have tended to minimise our symbols almost to the point of killing their significance.

❖ sacraments – ends or beginnings

Number six in our list of tensions or difficulties concerns the different understanding of what sacraments are. For many people they are seen as end-points. In fact, they also are beginnings. The Church has long talked about faith as a journey. On that journey we are continually renewed and refreshed. Every sacrament is thus a beginning of a new stage of this continual pilgrimage, not an end. Unfortunately, this is not always understood. Many a young person sees confirmation as an "exit point" for regular church attendance rather than as the beginning. Sometimes even our catechesis enforces this view because we place all our energies into *preparation* for a particular sacrament with little or no post-sacramental work. We shall return to this point in another section.

A final difficulty concerns how we see ourselves. If we are all on a journey of faith then we are a community of searchers, always discovering the life which God wishes us to live and the new awareness of God's presence within and amongst us. At the same time the Church is the custodian of the rich heritage of all that has been revealed. We have a treasury full of wealth which we must guard, respect and pass on. We live with the tension of being a custodian of the Church's riches and an explorer. Custodians tend to want to stand still and be protective, explorers want to move

custodian and explorer

> "Interpreting and illuminating experience with the data of faith is a constant task of catechetical pedagogy – even if with difficulty. It is a task that cannot be overlooked without falling into artificial juxtapositions or closed understandings. It is made possible, however, by a correct application of the co-relation and inter-action between profound human experiences and the revealed message."
>
> General Directory for Catechesis, 153

on and discover new avenues. These two are not mutually exclusive but keeping them in balance is not always easy. We tend to easily overbalance one way or the other.

So where does all this leave us? It is clear there are many tensions and many bridges to be built if people are to hear and experience good news through the sacraments of initiation. A question we may well ask ourselves is, through our sacramental life do people experience the good news which liberates them? Is their experience life giving? Do they discover (or rediscover) a living God? If they do then we may well be on the right track but if, as often seems to be the case, we see little or no sign of this then something is going wrong. God may well be calling us to look afresh at the way we celebrate these sacraments so that they do bring good news.

good news?

Pause & Reflect

What tensions do you experience with regard to your parish's preparation for and celebration of the sacraments of initiation? Do people experience your celebrations as good news for them?

2 WHAT MIGHT GOD BE SAYING?

Perhaps the first thing God might be saying to us in our present situation, with all our tensions and difficulties, is to take a new look at tension itself because it has the potential to be creative as well as destructive.

creative tension

Faced with tension our instinct is often to smooth things over but sometimes it can be the catalyst that makes us think and explore. It can be the spur to moving us onwards and sometimes it can jolt us into considering new possibilities. Sometimes it is the voice of God calling us forward.

gift not reward

One of the tensions we looked at in the previous section was that the sacraments are often seen as ends not beginnings. Along with that goes the idea that they are rewards rather than gifts. God has been at work in people long, long before we ever meet them or they meet us. They are not empty bottles to be filled with knowledge and then to receive the sacraments. Rather sacraments are a celebration of where God has led and is leading them. And they are God's freely given gifts; not earned or merited but given out of love. Of course such love requires a response but it is a response born out of gratitude and love in return for love. This is not easily understood or accepted in a culture in which "there is no such thing as a free lunch". Indeed it is a counter-cultural vision. Perhaps God is saying to us that wherever people are coming from and whatever their experience and motives, we should encourage them, and remind ourselves, that the sacraments are gifts not rewards. This will affect how we prepare and how we nurture.

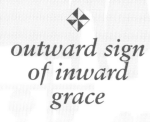

outward sign of inward grace

This inner work of God leads us to see these sacraments as a means of grace which are definitive moments but within the context of God's continuing action in each of us. God could be calling us to look afresh at how we can celebrate these sacraments as particular moments of grace *within* the continuum of God's action. We have a powerful example for this in the RCIA process. It reinforces the uniqueness of the sacramental moment; the outward sign of the inward grace of God's action.

"The rite of initiation is suited to a spiritual journey that varies according to the many forms of God's grace, the free co-operation of the individuals, the action of the Church and the circumstances of time and place."

Rite of Christian Initiation of Adults, 5

The real practice and experience in the parish with regard to these sacraments is often full of tension. Our deepest belief is that what these sacraments should be are moments of glory for people, beginnings of the journey. Our experience, however, is of people coming, "taking the sacraments" and then never seeing them again. This leaves us with a real sense of bewilderment, discouragement and sometimes anger. Many a priest or catechist knows the depression and hurt that arises from a feeling that we are simply not connecting. Indeed, we can sometimes feel really broken by the experience.

There is something deeply theological here. Brokenness is actually central to our faith. We believe in a Lord who came to triumph *through* brokenness. Can we expect anything else?

This brokenness, far from being negative, can, if we reflect on it, be a way forward for us. Firstly, we and the people we work with are *all* broken. It is part of what it means to be human. We share this with each other. Secondly, God shares this brokenness with us; God is the God of the broken, the poor. Thirdly, the Church itself is broken. Our membership of the Church is membership of the broken body of Christ – a Church which is Holy, Catholic and Apostolic but still bearing the wounds of the crucified Christ. So what are we initiating people into? We are inviting people to experience the all-powerful, risen and triumphant Lord but who is to be discovered in the weakness, the brokenness and the pain of our inner and outer world.

> *"(The catechist) must come to Christ with his unrest and uncertainty and even his weakness and sinfulness, his life and death. He must, so to speak, enter into Christ with all his own self, he must 'appropriate' Christ and assimilate the whole of the reality of the Incarnation and Redemption."*
>
> Catechesis in Our Time, 61

This is a very difficult concept for us and for others to grasp in a culture which prizes success, wealth and power, but it may open new avenues for all of us to realise afresh that we are initiated into the life of the wounded healer. It may well change the way we approach these sacraments both personally and as a Church community meeting those who come to us with all their own complexity and bewilderment.

This power of the sacraments to offer strength in weakness can only be described as a mystery. This word is much misunderstood. For most people mystery means a puzzle. To solve a puzzle we stand outside it and try to fathom it out. But this is not what Christianity

*recovering
the symbolic*

means by the word mystery. We "enter into the mystery of God". In other words we are being open to truths that are always there and beginning to glimpse their meaning. We enter the Christian mystery in order to begin to plumb its depths to discover it from within.

So celebrating a sacrament is to enter the mystery, the reality of God. This reality into which we are initiated in a new way at Baptism, First Confirmation and Communion should thus be a deepening experience of being in relationship with the crucified and risen Lord. A lot of our work around these sacraments concerns cognitive understanding – and quite rightly so – but perhaps we are being prompted to encourage each other, and those with whom we work, to discover with hearts as well as minds the mystery of God.

The life of God within and between us can be talked about, thought about and seen in all sorts of different ways. Because we are dealing with deep and profound issues that affect the very core of our being, one of the most natural means of expression for this encounter with God is the symbolic. We have already seen some of the difficulties with our symbolic world. Some are misunderstood or not understood at all. They mean little or nothing but that does not mean they are incapable of being recovered. Some "sacramentals" have already received new impetus or are commonly accepted (e.g. candles, flowers). Our sacramental symbols, water, oil, bread, wine, touch, are by no means dead but we do need to find new ways of enabling people to encounter their meaning. This means more than just explaining, which can sometimes do more harm than good. Symbols by their nature speak without words. It means letting people discover for themselves what these symbols say, not only to them personally, but to the community into which they are being initiated. Indeed the community into which people are initiated is itself a symbol. We are symbols for each other which affect the way we live and act – or should.

All of this paints a much more positive picture than we might have at first supposed. God offers us many an open door to explore the reality for today of what the Church has always known and experienced; that these sacraments are life-giving to a broken people and have the power to effect change within us which is beyond our wildest dreams as we walk our continuous journey of faith. So how can we walk through some of those open doors?

Pause & Reflect

What symbols do you think speak most to people today – why?

How might the idea of initiation into "the broken body of Christ" help us in our work with people today?

3   WHAT MIGHT GOD BE ASKING US TO DO?

There are many stories in the gospels about Jesus restoring people to wholeness. There is one in particular which gives us some clues about how we might respond to the tensions we have already thought about concerning the Sacraments of Initiation. It is the story of the deaf man who was also unable to speak. The story begins with Jesus returning from Tyre and moving towards the Sea of Galilee. It is on this journey that he is met by a group of people who bring a deaf man to him. This is our starting point.

> *Then he returned from the region of Tyre, and went by way of Sidon towards the Sea of Galilee, in the region of the Decapolis. They brought to him a deaf man who had an impediment in his speech; and they begged him to lay his hand on him.*
>
> (Mark 7:31-32)

Both Jesus and the man with his companions are on a journey. It is important that we remember that it is not only those who come to us, or are brought for the sacraments, who are engaging in a faith pilgrimage. So is the Church. We all are. This should affect the way the encounter happens.

Q   What difference does knowing we are all on a journey make to the way we prepare for and celebrate these sacraments?

Next, the people beg Jesus to lay his hands on the man. This is no half-hearted approach. They truly want what is best for their friend. They really want Jesus to do something. We have seen how the range of reasons for people coming for the sacraments is enormous and how basically they are expressing a deep-seated need. We have to acknowledge this variety of motivations and work with them.

on the journey "towards the Sea of Galilee"

"they begged Jesus"

Q   What is our reaction when people come and beg the sacraments from us?
How might we respond?

The next part of the story has Jesus taking the man aside, anointing him and speaking words to him.

He took him aside in private, away from the crowd, and put his fingers into his ears, and he spat and touched his tongue. Then looking up to heaven, he sighed and said to him, "Ephphatha," that is, "Be opened."

(Mark 7:33-34)

❖

sacramental action ... "he put his fingers into his ears"

Jesus does three things here. He *touches* him, he *uses* something (in this case spittle, well known for its healing properties) and he *speaks*. This is a sacramental action. The man would know that spit was symbolic of healing. The touch and the action would have spoken volumes to a man who could not hear. There are many people, within and outside our churches, who "cannot hear" our words. We have already mentioned the language problem and there are many who may well not be able to comprehend our symbolic action either. This was not the case for the deaf man. Jesus' act was one which itself spoke. The words came at the end. Maybe one of the ways forward is for us to look again at what symbols we could use *before* people receive these sacraments. What sacramentals are there which will awaken the symbolic for them?

Q   How can we explore *all aspects* of the sacraments, including touch, objects and words, in order to enrich our experience? What sacramentals might be appropriate?

After Jesus has acted we see the results of the action.
And immediately his ears were opened, his tongue was released and he spoke plainly.

(Mark 7:35)

❖

change ... "his ears were opened"

The man is changed but he is *still the same person*. Sacraments, as we have seen, are celebrations of God's action within us; high points which enable us to enter more deeply into the mystery of God's healing love. They do change us, or at least they should, but they are part of our continuing journey; they are points of departure. This means a new phase of life, a beginning not an end.

Q How can we help ourselves and others to see sacraments as points of departure rather than ends?

The final part of the story has Jesus ordering the man not to talk to anyone; an order which was disobeyed. The reaction of those around was astonishment.

> *Then Jesus ordered them to tell no one; but the more he ordered them, the more zealously they proclaimed it. They were astounded beyond measure, saying, "He has done everything well; he even makes the deaf to hear and the mute to speak."*
>
> (Mark 7:36-37)

Jesus' order to keep quiet is something especially strong in Mark's gospel. Jesus does not want people thinking he is a wonder-worker. Nor does he want to antagonise the authorities. But his action and his words are so radical that everyone talks about him. Things change when he is around, he "does everything well" and, because he does everything well, people know what it means to be really alive. Can we say this of our sacramental life? The challenge to us is that this story suggests that the only way for these sacraments to be as life giving as God intends them to be is if they are the focus of a radical following of Jesus. Where they are lived and celebrated by a community of people whose hearts and actions are part of radical discipleship, there power is enabled to flow in a way of which we might never have dreamt.

Q What does it mean to be a radical follower of Jesus? Doing everything well is more than just the *way* things are done. It relies on the spirit in which things are done. How does this challenge us to change?

We have explored a gospel passage here, as in other sections. We must not forget that the Word itself is "sacramental", that it has power to enable us to encounter the mystery of God in our own lives both individually and as a community. We have some real practical difficulties about celebrating the sacraments of initiation with some people. Indeed some, such as the divorced and re-married, cannot celebrate them due to the situations in which they find themselves, but the Word can be celebrated. Not only this, but the Word is an

❖

*radical following...
"he does everything well"*

❖

using the Word

> *"The gospel is the mouth of Christ. We are ministers of the Word, not our own word but the Word of our God and Lord. It is the Lord our God, Jesus Christ himself, who says to us what we have heard just now in the gospel. In explaining the holy Scriptures to you, I am, as it were, breaking and sharing bread with you. What I share out with you comes from the same storehouse in heaven: the common store is the Word of God."*
>
> St Augustine, Sermon 45

integral part of our sacramental life. However, it is not always seen as such. It is the Word of God. An avenue well worth exploring is how we can open up its richness to those who are forever on the threshold of our sacramental life. How can we enable ourselves and others to encounter God through the Word – and realise that this is a *real* encounter not a build-up or preparation for the "sacramental bit"?

Perhaps one of the reasons why we have not explored this as fully as we might has been that we tend to feel somewhat unhappy if we are not giving a sacrament. Why? Does it psychologically make us feel safer and less vulnerable if we engage in sacramental actions? Do we have a deep seated worry that if we don't do this fairly swiftly with people who come to us, we don't know what else to do?

Q What ways are there to encourage an enriched encounter with the Word?
How would this help those "on the threshold"?
What else might help them?

When Jesus and the deaf man met each other it was not planned, the time was right. For us in our parishes we do have planned times and seasons for sacramental initiation. So when is the "right time", the best time for us to celebrate God's love through these actions?

WHEN IS THE RIGHT TIME?

"But I will stay in Ephesus until Pentecost for a wide door for effective work has opened to me ..." (1 Corinthians 16:8)

At the time Rebecca was preparing for her First Communion her cousin Matthew was about to begin his Confirmation preparation. Matthew had always been involved in the life of the Church. Paul and Anne, Matthew's parents, were the only regular "practising Catholics" of Tom and Mary's close family. It was Anne's decision to become a Catholic through the RCIA process which had been the catalyst for Paul's new found interest. He had found that being with Anne through the process had rejuvenated his own faith.

Now Paul and Anne were unsure about whether Matthew was really ready for the reception of this particular sacrament. For Anne her own Confirmation as an adult had meant a great deal. Paul could hardly remember his apart from the "Bishop's tap on the cheek" and the choice of a new name. Would it not be better for Matthew to wait until he was older and make an informed choice based on a commitment which he could make as a young adult? On the other hand, Paul and Anne knew that Confirmation was linked to Baptism and perhaps this completion of initiation was better received before the traumas of adolescence set in with a vengeance.

For Matthew, like most young people in their early teens, Confirmation was something you did though he didn't clearly know why. After all nothing different seemed to happen afterwards – not like First Communion where there was a clear before and after. Although he would not say this to his parents, his image of Confirmation was that it was "the end". Thereafter he could make up his own mind about going to church, which he did not find particularly relevant. His two friends, Robert and Mark, were also to be Confirmed and so it was just what happened to most people in the group he belonged to. Matthew was very sure that he wanted to be like his friends, not different. He had a sneaking regard for James, the other member of the gang, who had decided to be Confirmed a year early. Poor James had had a bit of a rough time of it with his friends, but he had stuck to his guns and stubbornly insisted that he wanted to and didn't see why he should wait. Perhaps Matthew should stand up and be different too and decide to wait, or to say he simply didn't want to be Confirmed. But then Confirmation was not something Matthew felt important enough to raise a fuss about.

What Matthew did not know was that Paul and Anne had decided to discuss it all with him. When he got back from football on Saturday Paul mentioned it.

"Do you want to be Confirmed, Matthew?" he asked, getting milk out of the fridge. Matthew shrugged.

"All of my friends are," he replied.

"Except James," said Paul. "He made up his own mind. You should too."

"This is to be your choice, not ours. We won't pressurise you one way or the other," added Anne.

Matthew turned his dark brown eyes on his parents, "I don't know what it means really," he said.

"Then you must make up your mind when you do," said Anne, "and not before."

Matthew grinned, "OK," he said, "I'll let you know. Can James come round tomorrow after tea?"

"Sure," said Paul.

Pause & Reflect

What is your experience of how we decide when is the right time to celebrate the sacraments of initiation?

I LOOKING AT OUR SITUATION

As we have seen in previous sections the society in which we now live is one in which we expect to change and to change frequently. We no longer think things will stay the same for long. We are always moving on, often quite rapidly. This continuous ebb and flow means that we are no longer surprised if we go abroad for a fortnight and return to find the news has moved so fast it is almost impossible to discover what was responsible for the changes which have taken place. Yesterday's news is not news.

In addition to rapid changes in most areas of our lives we might also note that the stable patterns we once assumed were there for ever are also continuously changing. We see this in all sorts of ways. Here are three examples.

Patterns of relationships have changed and are continuously changing. Whatever our moral stance may be, we now know the chances are that most couples in our society will live together before they get married – if they ever get married at all.

Another example concerns the time at which couples decide to have children. The pattern has changed to having fewer children later on. Other changes in family life include single parenthood, which is more common for many reasons, and the number of people caring for elderly dependants has also increased as we all live longer.

rapid change

no stable pattern

A third example concerns the roles people play. Unlike previous generations, women may now choose to remain unmarried and follow careers of their own. We know men are rediscovering their role as partners in bringing up children and that in many a household two salaries are necessary to keep a roof over the family's head. Other people have roles thrust on them which limits their choice and this adds to the divisions within society. Some of us are able to choose, others cannot.

In addition to this change in former "stable" patterns, there is an increased awareness of individual development which means we are more flexible about times and ages. Although we retain basic guidelines about when things happen – for instance, ages for going to and leaving school and university – these and other basics are open to far more flexibility today. It is possible to obtain a university degree in retirement or to take exams early. This is not confined to education. Career changes half way through a working life, retraining or taking time out for all sorts of reasons are not uncommon. This is now in our consciousness as well as in our experience. We expect as much flexibility as possible in many areas of our lives.

Some people simply have no choice about either what or when they will do things because outside constraints prevent them. One of the characteristics of our society, however, is the assumption that individuals can now often decide, not only *what* they will do, but *when* they will do it.

All this means that in the Church we should not be surprised to find similar realities and tensions in our situation. Our previously stable pattern when everyone did everything at a specific time and age no longer works as well as it did. Now we are living in a world in which the questions "shall we, shan't we, are we ready, shall we wait?" are common for us in many areas of our lives. The question which then arises is, can the previously stable Catholic pattern for celebrating the sacraments of initiation be viable any longer or should we be exploring what a flexible pattern of ages would mean for us?

The other side of the flexibility coin is, of course, that it is much easier to stick with the pattern we know and which others expect. Like the tension between the Church as guardian of tradition and explorer on the faith journey which we considered earlier, there is a tension here between our desire to ensure people are able to respond

flexible about time and changes

a viable pattern

we want it now

47

appropriately to the gift God offers and the expectation of many people that this has always happened at a certain age and should stay that way. This surprisingly is tied up with the desire of our society for instant gratification. We want things and we want them now. So, if we want our child to make her or his First Communion at the same age we did, that is what we demand and that is what we expect to get. We must remember, however, parents want their child to receive First Communion at the same age as they did for other reasons. For many, especially non-practising Catholics, this set pattern provides a point of reference with the past, a reinforcing of their identity as Catholics. So, we must not dismiss the old patterns easily. They provide an anchor in a very insecure world. The question for every parish is how we handle both the desire for security and the knowledge that the old patterns are not working as well as they did.

Pause & Reflect

What changes in society do you see where a flexible approach to *when* we do things has had positive results?

2 WHAT MIGHT GOD BE SAYING?

In this changing and rapidly moving society what might God be saying to us about discerning the right time for the sacraments of initiation to be celebrated?

There are two major points to be considered here. One is about how we see initiation itself because this affects when we celebrate, and the other is about how we view time.

At present the Church has two tracks for initiation. RCIA for adults and a rite of Baptism for infants. There are historical reasons for both processes. It was important for early Christians to be aware of what they were taking on so there was a long, arduous process initiating them into a persecuted group who lived in a distinctive way opposed to the standards of the world around it. Later on the Church was no longer persecuted. Church and society were co-terminous. The emphasis was on being part of a Christian community and society and being saved from the state of original sin was a way into not only the Church but society itself.

two tracks

Neither of these historical experiences matches exactly our experience today. In Britain we are no longer a persecuted minority but neither are we dovetailed into society in the way the medieval church once was. We need a "third way".

To help us discover what this third way might be we need to look afresh where initiation fits in to the rest of our life.

all life is initiatory

In a very real sense all life is initiatory. Every time something new happens to us, good or bad, or we enter a new way of life, or a new job or a new relationship, we are being initiated into something and then we live that new life. Even our death will be initiatory. One of our difficulties is that we tend to see the sacraments of initiation as "one offs". And they are. The sacraments *are* definitive moments of God's grace but they are also to be lived out. We speak about living out our Baptism or living the Eucharist. An imperfect analogy comes from our knowledge of space. A comet plunges through space, unique and powerful, but as it does so it leaves behind its tail. That tail is made up of the same matter

> *"For all the baptised, children or adults, faith must grow after Baptism. For this reason the Church celebrates each year at the Easter Vigil the renewal of baptismal promises. Preparation for Baptism leads only to the threshold of new life. Baptism is the source of that new life in Christ from which the entire Christian life springs forth."*
>
> Catechism of the Catholic Church, 1254

as the head of the comet. In our sacramental life we experience these definitive moments of God's grace plunging into the depths of our lives but we also live continuously "in the tail". This is God's grace; it is on the same continuum and in it we live and move and have our being. So the whole of our life and time is in this initiatory cycle. God is always deepening our initiation into the life of the Trinity.

life stage and sacraments

Seeing God as always deepening our initiation gives us a different slant on how we understand time. Because these sacraments have generally been celebrated at a certain age, they have frequently become associated with the turning points between different stages of human life and development. For example, celebration of Confirmation at the onset of adolescence has often linked it closely to a new stage

> *"Age of body does not determine age of soul. Even in childhood man can attain spiritual maturity: as the Book of Wisdom says 'For old age is not honoured for length of time, or measured by number of years'. Many children, through the strength of the Holy Spirit they have received, have bravely fought for Christ even to the shedding of their blood."*
>
> St Thomas of Aquinas, STh III, 72, 8, ad 2; cf Wisdom 4:8
> quoted in Catechism of the Catholic Church, 1308

of life. In this way it becomes a celebration of the transition from childhood to maturity. The sacrament becomes a Rite of Passage not only in terms of people's faith development, but also in terms of human development. But if God is always deepening our initiation we find ourselves having to think differently. A faith journey is not necessarily "going at the same speed" as our educational or physical or psychological journeys. So linking the celebration of the sacraments with rites of passage might not be helpful. People will be at different stages of faith so *when* we celebrate needs careful thought. Discerning when people are ready, and helping them discern their own readiness, then becomes an important issue. Here we need to think a little about how our tradition sees the whole meaning of time and faith journey.

time

We frequently hear the expression "in God's good time". It's a phrase which shows that we realise that God's time is not necessarily the same as ours. There is human time and God's time. Sometimes they go together, sometimes they don't. There are two words for time in the Scriptures. One (*chronos*) means literally minutes and hours, that is time as we usually think about it. The other (*kairos*) is about God's moment, God's time. This is not so much about a succession of moments as about living in God's kingdom. Time and eternity are not separate. We live now in God's kingdom, in God's eternity, which is always beyond us and yet within and amongst us. So each of our moments in the process of time can be a *kairos*, a moment which either hastens or delays God's work within us. This makes every moment sacred.

To put it another way, there are occasions in all our lives when "time stands still" or "hangs heavy" or "flies". There are even moments when the past seems to be in the present, or when something happens that changes us radically in a few seconds. When we think about God's moment we need to be thinking along similar lines. In God's time the past, the present and the future are not separate so each moment can be described as "sacramental" because in each moment God is present. Alongside these we have the sacraments which are specific *kairos* moments.

discerning the kairos moment

When we think about sacramental initiation in this context it means that one of our responsibilities is to discern God's moment in the lives of those who are seeking these sacraments. Some people will themselves know when that moment has come, even if the chronological age does not fit into our normal pattern.

Pause & Reflect

When have you experienced "God's good time" in your own life?

One of the major ideas in the Scriptures to do with time is the stress on waiting. We are exhorted to wait for the moment, to seek and look for the right time when Jesus will be revealed – and this is not just to do with Jesus' second coming. This idea of waiting is one we might profitably explore in our contact with people coming for the sacraments. In the Church we live in a time of anticipation – or we should live that way. Always expecting the *kairos* moment to break through, always expecting God to be seen in and through our life at different moments in our own personal and community history. Encouraging people to wait expectantly is not simply a delaying tactic. It can be a theological and psychological time of growth. Individuals vary in their readiness and preparedness for the sacraments. We need to respect this and give them waiting time even if this means they spend all their lives on the threshold. Of course, all this is less neat and tidy than we might wish. It also calls into question *how* we should respond given the cultural and psychological pressures to resist change to our present practices.

❖

waiting is important

3 WHAT MIGHT GOD BE ASKING US TO DO?

In three of the four gospels we have the story which we know as the parable of the sower. Here is Mark's version.

(Jesus) began to teach them many things in parables, and in his teaching he said to them: "Listen! A sower went out to sow. And as he sowed, some seed fell on the path and the birds came and ate it up. Other seed fell on rocky ground, where it did not have much soil, and it sprang up quickly, since it had no depth of soil. And when the sun rose, it was scorched; and since it had no root, it withered away. Other seed fell among thorns, and the thorns grew up and choked it, and it yielded no grain. Other seed fell into good soil and brought forth grain, growing up and increasing and yielding thirty and sixty and a hundredfold." And he said, "Let anyone with ears to hear listen!"

(Mark 4:2-9)

every seed has potential

Looking at this very familiar story might help us discern how we might respond to the questions which surround the subject of when the sacraments should be celebrated.

The first point we can note is that each seed has the potential to grow into what it was meant to be. There is no distinction between good seed and poor seed, only between good and poor soil. In this story every single grain has within it all it needs to develop given the right conditions.

Seeing that every person who requests the sacraments is a God-given gift to us is not always easy, but it is central to our discernment process. In God's good time the work of grace is active within them and each one, like each one of us, will have experiences of life and faith which have led to where they are now.

Pause & Reflect

How can discovering where people are on their faith journey help the seed of faith to grow?

we grow at different speeds

The second point to note is that some seeds never germinate. The parable uses picture language for this.

> *And as he sowed, some seed fell on the path and the birds came and ate it up.* (v4)

The rest grows at different speeds depending on the environment.

> *Other seed fell on rocky ground, where it did not have much soil, and it sprang up quickly, since it had no depth of soil. And when the sun rose, it was scorched; and since it had no root, it withered away.* (v5-6)

helping each seed to grow at the right time

There are innumerable reasons why people develop at different speeds on their faith journey and it is important that when they come to us we do not judge them regarding this. Some may have been fortunate to have had the experience of growing in soil which has been well worked, other have not. What is important is that we recognise these varying speeds. That may mean that we have to move away from our current practice of seeing our celebrations as rites of passage between different stages of human development. We will need to discern the most appropriate moment in each case. This does not mean that we cannot have a "normal" time for most people. We need this, but it does require an attitude of much greater flexibility.

With reference to children, there is considerable concern that the average age for First Communion is too young. Furthermore, there is a growing difference of opinion about where Confirmation fits into the process. Four different views have emerged. First there is

> *"Although Confirmation is sometimes called the 'sacrament of Christian maturity', we must not confuse adult faith with the adult age of natural growth, nor forget that the baptismal grace is a grace of free, unmerited election and does not need 'ratification' to become effective."*
>
> Catechism of the Catholic Church, 1308

the view that Confirmation should be celebrated at the same time as Baptism, (as the Eastern Church does). Secondly, there are those who hold that Confirmation should be celebrated after Baptism but before First Communion. Thirdly that it should be celebrated with Holy Communion. Finally, there is the view that it should be conferred in the years after First Holy Communion. The basic question, however, is not simply which is the best age so that everyone can fit into it, but what will help this seed to grow in this situation? There are bound to be differences.

Q   What would be the positive benefits to a more flexible approach to the timing of the celebration of the sacraments?

A third point to note from the parable is what happens to the seed which grows in good soil.
> *"Other seed fell into good soil and brought forth grain, growing up and increasing and yielding thirty and sixty and a hundredfold."*
> (v8)

It does not produce all its fruit at once. The growth continues throughout the life of the plant. It grows up and increases the yield as time goes on. The question for us is how can we co-operate with God more closely to enable this growth to happen in God's good time.

There are those in our Church who believe that the best way to enable the seed of faith to grow is to restore the sacraments of initiation back to their original order (Baptism, then Confirmation, then Eucharist) and that all three of these should be generally celebrated early in life. A return to the original order would not be

❖
continued growth

❖
which order?

> *"From the time of the apostles, becoming a Christian has been accomplished by a journey and initiation in several stages. This journey can be covered rapidly or slowly but certain essential elements will always have to be present: proclamation of the Word, acceptance of the Gospel entailing conversion, profession of faith, Baptism itself, the outpouring of the Holy Spirit and admission to Eucharistic communion."*
>
> Catechism of the Catholic Church, 1229

new. It is at the heart of the way adults are initiated. Theologically it makes sense for people to celebrate Eucharist as the "summit" of initiation.

It demands, of course, that thereafter we must nurture the growing seed. There are others who would prefer the more common order to remain with an older age for Confirmation in the belief that our initiation should be celebrated over a long period of time.

Q In the light of the parable what do you think should happen to ensure the seed yields fruit at the right time?

Jesus ends the parable by pleading with those who hear the story to really listen, to be open to the message.

listen

> *"And he said, "Let anyone with ears to hear listen!"* (v9)

In this phrase God pleads with us to really listen to him, to those who come to us, and to each other. As we debate this issue, whatever tracks we choose to adopt, the need to provide the good soil which will enable the seed to grow must lie at the heart of our decisions.

It is to preparation of that soil, namely our catechesis and nurture, that we must now turn.

WHAT ABOUT OUR CATECHESIS?

"Keep a guard over my mouth O Lord" (Psalm 141:3)

Tom and Mary's daughter-in-law, Anne, was a catechist. She had originally helped out with the First Communion programme but had recently taken over as Baptism co-ordinator for the parish. As such she was well aware of the different motives and standpoints which those coming for the Baptism of their children bring with them. She knew about the difficulties of

> *"Above all, one must begin by accepting adults where they are ... it is essential to keep in mind the specific adults with whom one is working, their cultural background, human and religious needs, their expectations, faith experiences and their potential."*
>
> Adult Catechesis in the Christian Community;
> Some Principles and Guidelines, 56

trying to affirm and encourage them and she knew too that other catechists were experiencing something similar. She felt a bit like Eeyore in Winnie the Pooh who, when asked how he was, replied, "Not very how. I don't seem to have felt very how for a long time."

It was difficult for Anne to put a finger on what was wrong with the catechesis the parish offered. She knew that blame could not simply be laid at the door of those coming for the sacraments, nor could it be placed solely with the catechetical process the parish offered. Many good things had happened. There were positive stories in the parish of people who had stepped over the threshold and now fully shared the life of the local church. Yet there were also many stories of people coming, undergoing catechesis and never being seen again. This applied to all the sacraments of initiation.

At the meeting of catechists – which the parish held frequently – Anne raised some of her disquiet. Most of her colleagues agreed with her but no one had any concrete suggestions about what to do. Indeed it was quite difficult to get to grips with exactly what was wrong, but there was a general awareness that the catechesis their parish offered was not meeting the needs of those standing on the threshold, nor was it meeting the high ideals of what the parish thought catechesis should achieve.

Pause & Reflect

In what ways does the catechesis for the sacraments of initiation offered in your parish not feel "not very how"? Can you identify difficulties?

1 LOOKING AT OUR SITUATION

There are numerous reasons why we may be uncomfortable about the catechetical process we offer to those coming for the sacraments of initiation. Here are five primary ones.

varied starting places

Firstly we are meeting people who are often in an ambiguous relationship with the Church. Often they want to be identified with the Church but not to be active participants. As we have seen, they come with mixed motives, various expectations and at different stages on the faith journey. This makes catechesis more difficult, though as we shall see, there are some positive aspects to this situation.

> *"Initiatory catechesis ... comprises but surpasses mere instruction. Being essential, it looks for what is 'common' for the Christian ... being initiatory, it incorporates into the community, which lives, celebrates and bears witness to the faith."*
> General Directory for Catechesis, 68

Secondly, catechists are often unsure about how much people need to know. There are those in our community who say we do not give enough weight to teaching doctrine in our catechesis and those who say we give too much. The balance between the giving of information and the experience of what it means to grow in a faith relationship has to be kept together. We need both but there is always a tendency to overbalance one way or the other.

head and heart

> *RCIA 75 envisages initiation into not only the message but also the worship, witness and community of the local and universal Church – a faith formation "of a kind that while presenting Catholic teaching in its entirety also enlightens faith, directs the heart towards God, fosters participation in the liturgy, inspires apostolic activity and nurtures a life completely in accord with the spirit of Christ."*
> Rite of Christian Initiation of Adults, 78

Thirdly, there is the question of the relationship between liturgy and catechesis. We are sometimes unsure about this too.

Liturgy and catechesis are sometimes seen as totally separate. What experience of liturgy do we offer in our catechetical processes with adults and children? Do we offer the "rites" or do we offer living liturgy which symbolises and deepens faith? The experience of many suggests we do the former more often than the latter and that we do not give enough credit to the power of liturgy to educate and form people. This, of course, assumes a vibrant and living faith community.

liturgy and catechesis

home school parish

Fourthly, our experience in parish life makes us aware that the link between home, school and parish does not always operate as well as it might. In some places most catechesis operates through the school with little real link to the parish; in others it is offered through the parish but largely ignoring the school. In some parish and school have thought through the distinctive roles each can play but there is still the question of the home connection. This is often difficult because our history has led us to the point where the school is now seen by many parents to be the primary faith-educator of their children. They have, often through no fault of their own,

"The most commonly mentioned settings in which catechesis and religious education take place are the home, the parish and the school ... a greater partnership is called for between those who work in these settings."

Guidelines, 39

absorbed the belief that a Catholic schooling takes the place of faith education at home. This is not just a question of abrogating responsibility. It is often a genuine awareness by the parents of their own inadequacy or under-confidence in this area.

Finally, our situation tells us that a lot of people come for the sacraments of initiation and then disappear from our life as community. We make huge and costly efforts in the area of preparation, often demanding a great deal of those who stand on the threshold. We talk about these sacraments as a beginning but, unfortunately, we then offer little or nothing afterwards by way of continuing catechesis. There is far less emphasis on post-celebration catechesis compared to preparation. In many places there is little or no support or structure for nurturing the new life which we believe has been given. In others the structure is there but is rarely used. The result is that our message about the sacraments of initiation as beginnings is not backed up by our practice. Indeed, we give contradictory messages. To many people what should be the beginning is seen as the end because to all intents and purposes it *is* the end of a close connection with the faith community.

❖
what comes next?

Pause & Reflect

Which of the above five areas seems to you to be a priority for reflection in your own situation?

2 WHAT MIGHT GOD BE SAYING?

What then might be the message from God regarding our catechetical practice in the light of what we have discovered?

❖
opening doors

One of the things God might be encouraging us to do is to look honestly at our present practice. Does the local

"Catechesis must have a catechumenal style, as of integral formation rather than mere information: it must act in reality as a means of arousing true conversion."

General Directory for Catechesis, 29

where are they or where are we?

Church really open doors for people or does it lock them out? Doors can be opened for those who stand on the threshold in many ways; by the quality and vibrancy of the community life and by making sure that we use appropriate language and symbol. This has been mentioned before in this report, but its importance cannot be overstated. Using the right words and images can facilitate self discovery and lead to conversion. It broadens us out and enables us to see the Christian life as a combination of intellectual, spiritual, emotional and relational growth which affects the whole of us.

Another aspect of our catechetical processes which God might be asking us to look at afresh is the relationship between the catechesis of those requesting the sacraments of initiation and catechesis for all. It is not simply that we catechise others. We are all being catechised and we invite others to join our lifelong catechetical journey. Consequently, an important question for us to ask when people

> *"The Christian community not only gives much to those who are being catechised but also receives much from them ... Catechesis not only brings to maturity the faith of those being catechised but also brings the community itself to maturity."*
> General Directory for Catechesis, 221

stand on the threshold is not only "where are they" on their faith journey but "where are we" as a community on our faith pilgrimage? Just as we encourage those who stand on the threshold to grow in faith, so we should realise that we, as a faith community, are also called to mature and develop. We are helped in that process by those who join us. This process helps us mature as a faith community and leads us to new understandings.

respect God's catechetical activity

Linked to this is a need to be flexible in our catechetical approach. As we have already seen, God has been at work in the lives of those who come to us long before we ever meet them in a catechetical setting. We are not starting from scratch even though it may sometimes seem that way. One of the cardinal principles of catechesis is encouraging people to see where God has already acted in their lives. It is something we all need to do all the time. Christ already stands on the threshold with them, and with us as we meet them. Respecting that activity of God, using the awareness of it and leading on from it, requires an approach which realises we cannot simply put people through a programme regardless of their previous experiences. We need a framework but it must be flexible according to the needs we meet. Consequently we must resist the all too pervasive belief that we need to teach people everything. We are engaged on a journey. So some people will have already assimilated some truths, while others will be unable to take them on board at present.

Of course, this is far more untidy and difficult to manage than we might wish but it also has the advantage of releasing us from unnecessary pressures. We cannot, even if it was for the best, teach everything. Perhaps God is pointing us back to the wisdom of the early Church here, where the patristic model puts the celebration of the sacraments first and the explanations afterwards. Faith takes time to grow and mature. We cannot and should not try to do it all at once and should not crucify ourselves with unreal expectations. Discerning what to offer and what can wait is one of the hallmarks of a mature catechetical process. We can see this maturity of outlook and practice in a number of ways.

> *"Faith is a gift destined to grow in the hearts of believers. Adhering to Jesus Christ, in fact, sets in motion a process of continuing conversion, which lasts for the whole of life."*
>
> General Directory for Catechesis, 56

The first of these is that a mature person, or community, is one which is able to see and accept others as different from oneself. Maturity means, firstly, being able to understand that those who stand on the threshold, and many of those within the community, have different viewpoints and, secondly, to accept them with all these differences. Acceptance is where catechesis begins.

The second characteristic of maturity is that of respect for the dignity of the other. The respect of another's dignity means a refusal to patronise or talk down to them. It means acting and speaking with integrity. Sometimes respecting people may require that we let them go away from us without rancour, knowing that seeds have been faithfully sown and that we may not see the outcome. This requires that we have faith in God's continuing action within those who turn away from the threshold.

A third characteristic of maturity is a willingness to accept our own brokenness and poverty. Catechesis *is* about offering the great truths of our faith, it *is* about clarity of teaching and the challenge that comes with it. We *do* have a gospel to proclaim but part of that teaching is that growth comes from brokenness and resurrection comes through crucifixion. In so many of our communities we are often crucified by our inability to provide what we see as "good

◆

we cannot teach everything

◆

mature catechesis – respecting differences

– letting go in faith

– accepting brokenness

catechesis" or by the brokenness of our faith community which does not live up to the standards of the gospel. Yet our awareness of our brokenness is also a sign of our maturity as a people. It keeps us humble, it speaks to us as a challenge to move forward, it can also be a salutary reminder that we are still on the journey and, finally, it can often speak to others. They stand on our broken threshold with their own experiences of failure and brokenness. Recognising the brokenness of us both is a sign of maturity. God is able to do wonders where the doors of our catechesis are open to the prompting of the Spirit. If we are self sufficient, believing ourselves to be mature with nothing to learn, God can do little or nothing with us. Such an attitude closes us off from the often uncomfortable and, indeed, shocking revelations the Spirit brings.

Pause & Reflect

What signs of maturity can you see in the catechetical process offered in your own parish?
What might God be asking?

3   WHAT MIGHT GOD BE ASKING US TO DO?

How can we develop mature catechetical processes in our parishes when we are faced with those who come for the sacraments of initiation and who stand on the threshold with us?

In his meeting with the rich young man we are given a glimpse of how Jesus "catechised". It is a model we do well to explore. The story is recorded for us in Matthew, Luke and Mark. Here is the story from Mark.

As Jesus was setting out on a journey, a man ran up and knelt before him, and asked him, "Good Teacher, what must I do to inherit eternal life?" Jesus said to him, "Why do you call me good? No one is good but God alone. You know the commandments: you shall not murder; you shall not commit adultery; you shall not steal; you shall not bear false witness; you shall not defraud; honour your father and mother." He said to him, "Teacher, I have kept all these since my youth." Jesus, looking at him, loved him and said, "You lack one thing; go, sell what you own, and give the money to the poor, and

*you will have treasure in heaven; then come, follow me."
When he heard this, he was shocked and went away grieving,
for he had many possessions.*

*Then Jesus looked around and said to his disciples, "How
hard it will be for those who have wealth to enter the kingdom
of God!" And the disciples were perplexed at these words. But
Jesus said to them again, "Children, how hard it is to enter the
kingdom of God! It is easier for a camel to go through the eye
of a needle than for someone who is rich to enter the kingdom
of God." They were greatly astounded and said to one another,
"Then who can be saved?" Jesus looked at them and said, "For
mortals it is impossible, but not for God; for God all things are
possible."*

(Mark 10:17-27)

We are told in this story that Jesus is setting out on a journey when
the man appears with his question. We know from the gospels that
Jesus travels the countryside and that others travel to meet him. It is
when a meeting takes place that things happen. Our catechesis really
happens when our journey as a faith community stands on the
threshold with those who have journeyed towards us, and we truly
meet one another not only physically, but in dialogue.

Dialogue is what happens in the first part of the story. It starts with
the question by the man, "What must I do to inherit eternal life?" It
is not so much the *content* of the question which is important here
but the fact that there is a searching question being asked. Jesus
makes no judgement about the question. He replies by asking one of
his own and by doing this he starts the process of deepening the
man's awareness. Indeed, Jesus reinforces this starting place by
affirming what the seeker already knows. "You know the
commandments." Helping people discover what is already known
and what God has already disclosed is a second important stage in
the catechetical process.

Q   How can we affirm people on their catechetical journey?

The next part of the dialogue highlights another vital part of
catechesis. The man states that he has done his best to follow the
commandments and the gospel records Jesus' reaction. "Teacher, I

❖

*journeys
which meet*

❖

*affirming
what is
known*

❖

*looking for
the good*

have kept all these from my youth. Jesus, looking at him, loved him." In this context the word to "look" means to look steadily or deeply into the heart. Jesus sees all the good this man has done. He *has* tried, he *has* wanted to do the best and, for all those attempts and the desires, Jesus loves him. There is no hint of condemnation or judgement that the man has not done enough. Jesus sees the good. Catechesis must affirm the good, helping people to see where they have been faithful to their best intentions. Above all effective catechesis is centred on our openness to look deeply into people and love them unconditionally.

Q   In what ways do we implicitly or explicitly judge people when they come into the catechetical process?
How can we affirm the good in them?

It is only after he has affirmed and acknowledged the worth of this young man that Jesus issues his challenge, "Go sell what you own, and give the money to the poor, and you will have treasure in heaven; then come, follow me." There is – or should be – an important challenge in our catechesis. It is an essential element but it is made in the context of affirmation and love. Only then can people make an informed choice.

Q   How do we challenge those who come to us in ways that enable them to respond positively?

In the gospel the response is negative. The man is unable to do what Jesus asks, "He was shocked and went away grieving". He did not drift away through lack of interest. He had been profoundly attracted to what he had seen and profoundly challenged. He leaves shocked at the enormity of the demand, but also sad at heart that he could not respond. And *Jesus lets him go.*

Our catechetical process should never be such that people drift away. It should attract and challenge. If the response is positive it will be because people have discovered an answer to their questions or they have found a community where they have discovered an experience of God's presence. If the response is negative we, like Jesus, should let them go. This letting go comes hard to us. We feel we have failed – and there may be some truth in that – but the story gives us a new

challenging in love

letting go

leave the door ajar

way of looking at those who turn away rather than cross over the threshold. When Jesus sees the young man leave he does not condemn him. His assessment of what has happened is left until he talks to the disciples. His teaching about wealth and possessions is to them *not* to the young man. By refusing to condemn him and by letting him go Jesus leaves the door ajar for a return. We do not know if the man does come back, just as we cannot know the future of those whose lives we touch, but the honest assessment of what has happened and the lack of harsh judgement has two effects. It means first of all that people can leave "without a bad taste in their mouths"; in other words, knowing a return is possible. Secondly, it makes us look hard at ourselves; it urges us to learn from what has happened, just as the disciples are encouraged to learn from what they have seen and heard.

Q How do we cope with the negative responses and how might we encourage people to return?

The final part of this passage concerns the conversation Jesus has with the disciples. Jesus has to reiterate his teaching. "How hard it will be for those who have wealth to enter the kingdom of God", but the disciples "were perplexed". So, Jesus has to try again, "Jesus said to them again, Children, how hard it is to enter the kingdom of God! It is easier for a camel to go through the eye of a needle than for someone who is rich to enter the kingdom of God". Even at the end of this explanation the disciples "were astounded" and talked about it among themselves. Jesus once again has to make a statement which he does "looking at them" – the same word used of Jesus looking deeply into the heart of the rich young man.

What is going on here is a process. It is what we might call post-event catechesis. Jesus is leading the disciples towards greater understanding *after* the incident has occurred. We have already noted that catechesis is life-long and the need for post-event catechesis. In the RCIA process it is called the period of deepening the mysteries, or mystagogia. This part of our catechetical life has been neglected for too long. This story encourages us to reassess the place of post-sacramental work

we learn after the event

> *Pope John Paul II speaks of "the 'rights' that each baptised person has to being instructed, educated and supported in the faith and the Christian life."*
>
> Christifideles Laici, 34

and to ask whether we have got the balance between pre- and post-sacramental catechesis right. It also encourages us to see that catechesis is always valid, even when reception of the sacraments is not possible for particular reasons.

Q   Where does the emphasis lie in your situation – on pre- or post-sacramental catechesis?
Should anything be changed and, if so, how?

When we look at this story we see a process. The disciples ask their questions and are willing to learn because they have been faced with a real life situation. Someone has come, a situation has arisen which requires an answer and Jesus has handled it. It has led them to continue their own search and engage in their own honest conversation with Jesus.

We are faced with people who stand on our threshold requiring an honest, loving response from us. What we do and say will either create a positive or a negative response. What we desire is that those who stand on the threshold will have the opportunity to respond positively to Jesus' invitation "Follow me" and join us in that continuing dialogue which leads us all into a greater understanding and experience of the God who is behind us, with us and before us on our faith journey.

motivation

> " 'The definitive aim of catechesis is to put people not only in touch, but also in communion and intimacy, with Jesus Christ.' All evangelising activity is understood as promoting communion with Jesus Christ ... catechesis seeks to solidify and mature this first adherence."
>
> General Directory for Catechesis, 80

Q   If you had to put down in one sentence your motivation for catechesis what would it be?

At the end of this incident, recorded for us in the gospels, Jesus gives a message of hope. No matter how hard the task, how difficult the challenge "for God all things are possible". To us has been given the privilege and the responsibility of journeying with those who come to the threshold of our Church asking for the sacraments of initiation. We are called to welcome, encourage and challenge them in the sure and certain hope that, whatever the outcome, "for God all things are possible".

FINAL REFLECTION

In this report we have often used the images of doorways and thresholds. A range of questions both spoken and unspoken lies behind these images. When individuals or families approach the parish community to seek the sacraments of initiation for themselves or their children will they find themselves facing a doorkeeper? Will this doorkeeper admit them, or will they find their way barred if they do not in some way fulfil the criteria of entry? Many parish priests and catechists have a sense that they have to fulfil this doorkeeping role.

What makes this image of the doorkeeper particularly uncomfortable – even disturbing – are the overtones of power and control that it sometimes carries and these overtones sit uneasily with the Gospel message of service and liberation. Those who request the sacraments may see priests and catechists as figures of authority and they may expect them to behave in a similar way to others they have encountered in charge of doorways – be it in the school, the workplace, the family or the benefits agency. Such experiences can colour people's attitudes as they come to the threshold of the Church – attitudes that can range from the very submissive to the outright belligerent. Responding in the right ways to these patterns of behaviour and attitudes is a challenge to every parish community. It demands of us all that we do three things. First, that we explore in a focussed way our own attitudes towards the world in which we live. Secondly, that we have a renewed sense of the meaning of these sacraments and, finally, that we look honestly at how we interact with others.

As we try to find a way through these complex encounters, it may be helpful to consider an image that Christ uses of himself:

> ... Jesus said, "Very truly, I tell you, I am the gate for the sheep. All who came before me are thieves and bandits; but the sheep did not listen to them. I am the gate. Whoever enters by me will be saved, and will come in and go out and find pasture. The thief comes only to steal and kill and destroy. I came that they may have life, and have it abundantly."
>
> (John 10:7-10)

Behind this passage there may lie the image of the little stone corral into which the shepherd of Jesus' time would gather his flock during

the night. Instead of a formal gateway, it simply had a hole in its perimeter wall through which the shepherd would guide his sheep in the evening, and across which he himself would lie through the hours of darkness. The protecting gate was his own body, over which those, both within and without, might easily trample. He stayed outside the security of the sheepfold and remained, vulnerable, on its threshold.

This image carries no overtones of power, but eloquently expresses some of the feelings of helplessness and insecurity experienced by many who work in parish catechesis. To be on the threshold with people is to share with them their hopes and anxieties, to listen carefully and generously as they unfold the story of their own insecurities, to attempt to help them to discern the right time. As we patiently remain there with others we become aware of the complexities of their situations. We also find ourselves awakened to our own uncertainties. Far from finding that the threshold is a place of easy solutions, ready answers and distinct conclusions, all parties can emerge from it with further questions and a sense of unease and incompleteness.

The threshold is above all a place of service – not only to those who approach, but also to the Lord who invites men and women to be members of his Body. Like Christ, we stand on the threshold as ones who serve. It is hoped that this report will be used as a resource for us to explore ways of acting not so much as all-powerful doorkeepers but as humble threshold-companions.

FULL TITLES OF THE MAJOR CHURCH DOCUMENTS AND TEXTS QUOTED IN THE REPORT

The Church in the Modern World (Gaudium et Spes)
Vatican II Pastoral Constitution – December 1965

Evangelisation in the Modern World (Evangelii Nuntiandi)
Pope Paul VI Apostolic Exhortation – December 1975

Catechesis in Our Time (Catechesi Tradendae)
Pope John Paul II Apostolic Exhortation – October 1979

Christifideles Laici
Pope John Paul II Apostolic Exhortation – 1986

Guidelines – Jim Gallagher SDB
Bishops' Conference of England and Wales, National Project of
Catechesis and Religious Education Document – 1986

Rite of Christian Initiation of Adults – 1987

Adult Catechesis in the Christian Community
International Council for Catechesis – 1990

Catechism of the Catholic Church – 1994 edition

General Directory for Catechesis – August 1997
Congregation for the Clergy – August 1997

Quotations from the Scriptures are taken from the New Revised
Standard Version – 1993

MEMBERSHIP OF THE WORKING PARTY

The eleven members of the Working Party represented a range of backgrounds and experience. The members were:

The Right Rev Brian Noble – Bishop of Shrewsbury; Chairman of the Bishops' Conference Pastoral Liturgy Committee

Rev Michael Cooke – Director of the Religious Education Centre, Diocese of Salford; Secretary to the Bishops' Conference Department for Education and Formation

Dr Christine Dodd – Adviser for Adult Education, Diocese of Hallam; Member of the Bishops' Conference Home Mission Committee and the RCIA National Network

*Rev Andrew Faley – Vice Rector of the Beda College, Rome; formerly National Adviser for Catechesis and Religious Education

Rev Nicholas Hudson – Director of the Christian Education Centre, Archdiocese of Southwark; Member of the RCIA National Network

*Miss Pat Jones – Deputy Director of CAFOD; formerly Assistant General Secretary of the Bishops' Conference

*Rev Liam Kelly – Assistant General Secretary to the Bishops' Conference

Mrs Suzanne Kowal – Adviser for Parish Catechesis and Adult Formation, Diocese of Plymouth; Member of the RCIA National Network

Rev Peter McGrail – Director of the Department of Pastoral Formation, Archdiocese of Liverpool; Member of the Bishops' Conference Church Music Committee

Rev Brian Newns – Parish Priest, Archdiocese of Liverpool

*Rev David Oakley – Lecturer in Pastoral Theology, Oscott College, Archdiocese of Birmingham

Most members were able to participate throughout the life of the Working Party. Those who were only able to be present for part of the process are marked with an asterisk.